Will

What Has Athens to Do with Jerusalem?

By his will, Mr. Thomas Spencer Jerome endowed the lectureship that bears his name. It is jointly administered by the University of Michigan and the American Academy in Rome, and the lectures for which it provides are delivered at both institutions. They deal with phases of the history or culture of the Romans or of peoples included in the Roman Empire.

F. E. Adcock, *Roman Political Ideas and Practice*

G. W. Bowersock, *Hellenism in Late Antiquity*

Frank E. Brown, *Cosa: The Making of a Roman Town*

Jacqueline de Romilly, *The Rise and Fall of States According to Greek Authors*

Anthony Grafton, *Commerce with the Classics: Ancient Books and Renaissance Readers*

Claude Nicolet, *Space, Geography, and Politics in the Early Roman Empire*

Massimo Pallottino, *A History of Earliest Italy*

Jaroslav Pelikan, *What Has Athens to Do with Jerusalem?* Timaeus *and* Genesis *in Counterpoint*

Brunilde S. Ridgway, *Roman Copies of Greek Sculpture: The Problem of the Originals*

Lily Ross Taylor, *Roman Voting Assemblies: From the Hannibalic War to the Dictatorship of Caesar*

Mario Torelli, *Typology and Structure of Roman Historical Reliefs*

Paul Zanker, *The Power of Images in the Age of Augustus*

JEROME LECTURES, 21

What Has Athens to Do with Jerusalem?

Timaeus and *Genesis* in Counterpoint

Jaroslav Pelikan

Ann Arbor

THE UNIVERSITY OF MICHIGAN PRESS

Copyright © by the University of Michigan 1997
All rights reserved
Published in the United States of America by
The University of Michigan Press
Manufactured in the United States of America
⊗ Printed on acid-free paper

2000   1999   1998   1997   4   3   2   1

A CIP catalog record for this book is available from the British Library

Library of Congress Cataloging-in-Publication Data

Pelikan, Jaroslav Jan, 1923–
    What has Athens to do with Jerusalem? : Timaeus and Genesis in
counterpoint / Jaroslav Pelikan.
        p.   cm. — (Jerome lectures ; 21)
    Includes bibliographical references.
    ISBN 0-472-10807-7 (cloth : alk. paper)
        1. Plato. Timaeus.   2. Bible. Genesis—Comparative studies.
    3. Lucretius Carus, Titus. De rerum natura.   4. Cosmogony, Ancient.
    5. Creation—Biblical teaching.   6. Creation—History of doctrines.
    I. Title.   II. Series: Jerome lectures ; 21st ser.
    B387.P45   1997
    261.5′1—dc21   97-4244
                                                                    CIP

To Laurence,
who is οὐκ ἀσήμου πόλεως πολίτης (*Ac.* 21:39)—
indeed, a citizen of each of these cities

Preface

From 29 January to 7 February 1996 at the University of Michigan, and then from 15 to 24 April 1996 at the American Academy in Rome, I had the honor of being the thirtieth in the series of Thomas Spencer Jerome Lecturers. It is a delight to begin this printed version of the lectures by following the example of all my predecessors in the Jerome Lectureship in thanking my colleagues at both Ann Arbor and Rome for their kindness and hospitality, and for the special combination of incisiveness and unfailing courtesy with which they put their questions to me and carried on their discussions with me, thus enabling me to improve my exposition and strengthen my arguments. My investigations of these texts have taken me into some waters where I do not usually swim at these depths, in which yet other colleagues, in particular Professor Mary Lefkowitz of Wellesley College, have been my lifeguards, and occasionally my rescuers. Colin Day, Director of the University of Michigan Press, and Ellen Bauerle, my editor, have skillfully seen the project through to its completion, from when it was little more than a Platonic idea. Chapter 5 was not part of the original five Jerome Lectures, but was given a month later, on 21 May 1996, also in Rome, at the joint meeting of the Accademia dei Lincei and the American Philosophical Society. I have also had the opportunity of presenting some of this material on the distinguished platforms of the Lowell Lectures at Boston University and the Bradley Lectures at Boston College.

Contents

A Note on Translations

Almost all the thinkers with whom this book deals were obliged to read either *Timaeus* or *Genesis* or both in translation, the principal exceptions to this being those Hellenistic Jews who had kept a knowledge of Hebrew after acquiring Greek (which may or may not include Philo and the author or authors of the *Book of Wisdom*), as well as those few Christians, Origen and some others, who could read each of the two books in the original. Therefore the problem of translation, which has been vexing—and fascinating—me both personally and professionally throughout my life, has proved to be even more complex here than usual.

In performing the pleasant duty of working through the Greek text of *Timaeus* countless times for this assignment, I have had the benefit of various translations into various languages, above all that of Francis M. Cornford, which was the version I quoted most often in my early drafts. Then, for a while, I had come to the conclusion that I should, despite my reservations, revert to the translation of Benjamin Jowett in its fourth edition, for several reasons: it is by far the best known throughout the English-speaking world, and it is in many ways the most beautiful as literature; his renderings, by some of the very qualities that make them controversial, best prepare a reader for the interpretations imposed on *Timaeus* by later generations of Jews and Christians; and his was the version of *Timaeus* selected by Edith Hamilton and Huntington Cairns for their one-volume Bollingen edition of Plato (published in 1961 and several times since), despite the availability to them of the English *Timaeus* of Cornford, whose translations of *Theaetetus*, *Parmenides*, and *Sophist* they did include.

Nevertheless, despite personal preferences, I finally decided that to achieve consistency and avoid the impression of arbitrariness, I should adhere as much as I could to the translations of my various texts in the Loeb Classical Library and in the New English Bible (though without reproducing the verse forms and capital letters of the latter), at least for

direct quotations, often quoting the originals together with them. But I
have also felt free to add (or substitute) my own translations and para-
phrases (for example, of the key passage from *Timaeus* 92C throughout)
and even—particularly in the case of the English translation by Victor E.
Watts of the "Hymn to the Creator" from book 3 of the *Consolation of
Philosophy* of Boethius and in the case of a few key passages from Jowett
and from the Bible—to use some other existing English translations,
where their renderings come closer to the sense in which my two primary
texts, *Timaeus* and *Genesis,* were being interpreted by the later readers of
the two together. In some cases, those later interpreters may themselves
have influenced these translations, which is, for my purposes here, an asset
rather than a liability. I have also sought to be as consistent as I could in
reproducing the fundamental distinction of *Timaeus* between νοητός and
αἰσθητός with the translations "apprehensible only to the mind" and
"perceptible to the senses," deviating therefore from the practice of the
Loeb Classical Library, which often translates αἰσθητός with "sensible," a
meaning the term certainly would not have for most readers of English
today. For the Latin version of *Timaeus* by Calcidius, I have usually translated his translation, even where it is faulty or misleading. A similar crite-
rion has persuaded me, where an author is employing the Septuagint or
the Vulgate with a meaning that diverges significantly from the one reflected in the NEB (and, for that matter, from the original), to quote or
adapt English translations of those translations.

Abbreviations

Primary Sources

Ambr.	Ambrose of Milan
Exc. Sat.	De excessu fratris sui Satyri
Fid.	De fide
Hex.	Hexaemeron
Arist.	Aristotle
E.N.	Ethica Nicomachea
Met.	Metaphysica
Ph.	Physica
Ath.	Athanasius
Apol. sec.	Apologia (secunda) contra Arianos
Ar.	Orationes contra Arianos
Syn.	De synodis Arimini et Seleuciae
Aug.	Augustine
Civ.	De civitate Dei
Conf.	Confessiones
Corrept.	De correptione et gratia
Doct. christ.	De doctrina christiana
Gen. imp.	De Genesi ad litteram imperfectus liber
Gen. litt.	De Genesi ad litteram
Gen. Man.	De Genesi adversus Manichaeos
Trin.	De Trinitate
Bas.	Basil of Caesarea
Hex.	Homiliae in Hexaëmeron
Spir.	De Spiritu sancto
Boet.	Boethius
Cons.	De consolatione philosophiae

Div.	*Utrum pater et filius et spiritus sanctus de divinitate substantialiter praedicentur*
Eut.	*Contra Eutychen et Nestorium*
int.	Introduction
Herm. sec.	*In librum Aristotelis* περὶ ἑρμενείας *editio secunda*
pr.	Preface
Trin.	*De Trinitate*
pr.	Preface
Cal.	Calcidius
Com.	*Commentarius*
Ti.	*Timaeus*
ep. ded.	Dedicatory epistle
Cic. *Ti.*	Cicero *Timaeus*
Clem. *Str.*	Clement of Alexandria *Stromateis*
Gr. Naz.	Gregory Nazianzus
Ep.	*Epistolae*
Or.	*Orationes*
Gr. Nyss.	Gregory of Nyssa
Anim. res.	*De anima et resurrectione*
Beat.	*Orationes de beatitudinibus*
Cant.	*Homiliae in Cantica Canticorum*
Ep.	*Epistolae*
Eun.	*Contra Eunomium*
Hex.	*Apologia in Hexaëmeron*
Hom. opif.	*De opificio hominis*
ep. ded.	Dedicatory epistle
Maced.	*De Spiritu sancto contra Macedonianos*
Or. catech.	*Oratio catechetica*
Or. dom.	*Homiliae in orationem dominicam*
Ref.	*Refutatio confessionis Eunomii*
Tres dii	*Quod non sint tres dii*
V. Mos.	*De vita Mosis*
Hil. *Trin.*	Hilary of Poitiers *De Trinitate*
Hom. *Il.*	Homer *Ilias*

Hor. *Epist.*	Horace *Epistolae*
Iren. *Haer.*	Irenaeus of Lyons *Adversus haereses*
Just. *Dial.*	Justin Martyr *Dialogus cum Tryphone Judaeo*
Lact.	Lactantius
Epit.	*Epitome diuinarum institutionum*
Inst.	*Diuinae institutiones*
Lucr.	Lucretius *De rerum natura*
Or. *Cels.*	Origen *Contra Celsum*
Ov. *Met.*	Ovid *Metamorphoses*
Phil.	Philo of Alexandria
Cher.	*De cherubim*
Conf.	*De confusione linguarum*
Congr.	*De congressu eruditionis gratia*
Decal.	*De Decalogo*
Fug.	*De fuga et inventione*
Leg. all.	*Legum allegoria*
Migr.	*De migratione Abrahami*
Opif.	*De opificio mundi*
Quaes. Gen.	*Quaestiones et solutiones in Genesin*
V. Mos.	*De vita Mosis*
Pl.	Plato
Criti.	*Critias*
Leg.	*Leges*
Phd.	*Phaedo*
Resp.	*Respublica*
Tht.	*Theaetetus*
Ti.	*Timaeus*
Socr. *H.e.*	Socrates Scholasticus *Historia ecclesiastica*
Soz. *H.e.*	Sozomenus Salaminus *Historia ecclesiastica*
Tert.	Tertullian
Anim.	*De anima*
Marc.	*Adversus Marcionem*
Praescrip.	*De praescriptione haereticorum*

Verg.   Vergil
  Aen.   *Aeneis*
  Ecl.   *Eclogae*

Reference Works

Bauer   Bauer, Walter A. *A Greek-English Lexicon of the New Testament and Other Early Christian Literature.* Trans. and adapted by William F. Arndt, F. Wilbur Gingrich, and Frederick W. Danker. 2d ed. Chicago, 1979.

Blaise   Blaise, Albert. *Dictionnaire latin-français des auteurs chrétiens.* Brussels, 1975.

DTC   *Dictionnaire de théologie catholique.* 15 vols. Paris, 1903–50.

Lampe   Lampe, Geoffrey W.H., ed. *A Patristic Greek Lexicon.* Oxford, 1961.

LTK   *Lexikon für Theologie und Kirche.* 10 vols. and index. Freiburg, 1957–67.

OCD   *The Oxford Classical Dictionary.* 2d ed. Oxford, 1992.

PW   Pauly, A., G. Wissowa, and W. Kroll, eds., *Real-Encyclopädie der klassischen Altertumswissenschaft.* 1893–.

Tanner-Alberigo   Tanner, Norman P., and Joseph Alberigo, eds. *Decrees of the Ecumenical Councils.* London and Washington, 1990.

TLL   *Thesaurus Linguae Latinae.* Leipzig, 1900–.

I

Classical Rome: "Description of the Universe" (*Timaeus* 90E) as Philosophy

The Thomas Spencer Jerome Lectures are charged, by the will of their founder, to deal with (among other possible themes) "the history or culture of the Romans." Previous lecturers in this distinguished series have correctly construed that charge quite broadly, so as to include not only Roman "history or culture" in the classical period but its subsequent development into the Christian and Catholic period.[1] For the history or culture of the Romans became truly universal, and Rome became the "imperium sine fine" prophesied in Vergil's *Aeneid*,[2] not by the history of the Caesars alone but by the history of the popes as well, not only through the culture that spoke in the Latin of the *Aeneid* but also through the culture represented by the Latin of the Vulgate and the Mass. As Alexander Souter, editor of the *Glossary of Later Latin*, once put it, "it seems indisputable that, whether Augustine be the greatest Latin writer or not, he is the greatest man who ever wrote Latin."[3] This Latin culture of Catholic Rome dominated the history and culture of the Mediterranean world and of western Europe for more than a millennium and then spread from there to the seven continents and to the islands of the sea.

An important part of that process, both as a symbol and as an instrument of such universality, was the appropriation by Christian and Catholic Rome of titles as well as of themes that had originated in classical Rome and its forebears, a process that was justified as an analogy to the Israelites' having taken spoils from the Egyptians in the Exodus.[4] Among the titles, perhaps the most familiar is *pontifex maximus*, repeated hundreds of times on the monuments and plaques of present-day Rome: originally a title for the chief priest of Roman pagan religion, it was taken

---

1. Most notably, perhaps, Bowersock 1990.
2. Verg. *Aen.* 1.279.
3. Souter 1910, 150.
4. Aug. *Doct. christ.* 2.40.60–61.

over by the emperors during the principate of Augustus, was therefore renounced by the Christian emperors beginning with Gratian in the last quarter of the fourth century, but then was assumed (though not initially as an exclusive title) by the popes in the next century, beginning with Pope Leo I.[5] Among the themes taken over, the best known is probably the myth of the birth of the Child in Vergil's *Fourth Eclogue:* "Now the Virgin returns [Iam redit et Virgo]. . . . Now a new generation descends from heaven on high. Only do thou . . . smile on the birth of the child, under whom the iron brood shall first cease, and a golden race spring up throughout the world!"[6] Because of its striking similarities to the prophecy of the birth of the child in the *Book of Isaiah,* this was applied by many Christians to the birth of the Christ child.[7] Another such appropriation is reflected in the opening stanza of the *Dies irae,* "teste Dauid cum Sibylla."[8] In its use of both these Roman sources, which had been related to each other through the prominence in the *Fourth Eclogue* of the Cumaean Sibyl, as she and the other Sibyls were eventually to be memorialized in the Sistine Chapel in association with the prophets of Israel,[9] Catholic Rome set its classical heritage into a kind of counterpoint with its Jewish and biblical heritage—David into counterpoint with the Sibyl for Christian eschatology, Isaiah into counterpoint with the *Fourth Eclogue* for the messianic hope.

Almost as soon as Christianity had gone beyond Greek to speak and write in Latin, it began to raise fundamental questions about that counterpoint. "What has Athens to do with Jerusalem?" [Quid Athenae Hierosolymis?], asked Tertullian, the first important Latin Christian author.[10] The answer of Tertullian to his own question was that the faithful disciple of Jerusalem did not really need to become a pupil of Athens as well. In proof of that answer, however, he declared: "Our instruction comes from 'the porch of Solomon,' who had himself taught that the Lord should be 'sought in simplicity of heart.'"[11] Thus he quoted, in the same breath with

---

5. Max Bierbaum in *LTK* s.v.; Blaise 634.

6. Verg. *Ecl.* 4.6–10.

7. *Is.* 9:6; Norden 1924.

8. Arthur Stanley Pease in *OCD* s.v.; Emile Amann in *DTC* s.v.; Karl Prümm, Anton Legner, Johann Michl in *LTK* s.v.

9. Hersey 1993, 198–204.

10. Tert. *Praescrip.* 7; Cochrane 1944, 213–60, "Quid Athenae Hierosolymis? The Impasse of Constantinianism," is still a helpful examination.

11. *Wis.* 1:1.

the warning of the apostle Paul against "philosophy and empty deceit,"[12] the words of the first verse of the *Wisdom of Solomon,* in which the contrapuntal harmony between Athens and Jerusalem was more pronounced than in any other biblical book. The theme of that counterpoint in the *Book of Wisdom,* moreover, was not the conjunction of Isaiah and Vergil on the birth of the Child nor the conjunction of David and the Sibyl on the end of the world but the conjunction of *Genesis* and *Timaeus* on the beginning of the world. Having almost certainly been composed originally in Greek rather than in Hebrew, the *Wisdom of Solomon* is not only the most Hellenized but also arguably the most "philosophical" book in the Bible. That, too, was a reflection and an adumbration, for it would be as a philosophical-theological cosmogony that the combination of *Timaeus* and *Genesis* would present itself to Judaism in Alexandria and then to Christianity in New Rome and in Catholic Rome.

This book deals with that question of cosmogony, the doctrine of beginnings and of origins, as the question was posed for Roman culture from classical Rome to Catholic Rome by the counterpoint between the *Genesis* of Moses and the *Timaeus* of Plato. But in "the history or culture of the Romans" cosmogony had been the subject of myth and speculation quite apart from that counterpoint, most familiarly perhaps for readers of Latin literature past and present in book 1 of Ovid's *Metamorphoses.*[13] Ovid's poetic account of creation was, however, far less scientifically extensive and philosophically profound than that set forth in the *De rerum natura* of Lucretius. It seems fair to say that together with Dante Alighieri and Johann Wolfgang von Goethe, Lucretius represented a distinctive combination of poetry, science, and philosophy, which was why George Santayana bracketed him with those two later writers in his *Three Philosophical Poets* of 1910. Lucretius was well aware of his uniqueness within the Roman tradition, describing himself as a poet who followed the Muses on untrodden paths and traveled where none had gone before,[14] and identifying himself, with the words "denique natura haec rerum ratioque repertast / nuper, et hanc *primus cum primis ipse* repertus / nunc *ego sum* in patrias qui possim uertere uoces," as the first to have been in a position to give a full cosmological and cosmogonic account of the nature and

---

12. *Col.* 2:8.
13. Ov. *Met.* 1.5–88; I have benefited from the commentary of Bömer 1969, 15–47, in my reading of these lines.
14. Lucr. 1.922–27, 4.1–2.

system of the world in Latin, whether in poetry or in prose.[15] The epic of Lucretius is endlessly fascinating above all in its own right as the first full-length philosophical and scientific cosmogony we know of in Rome. But for the purposes of the present inquiry, it is valuable not primarily for its literary form or its scientific content but especially for its philosophical and theological *Fragestellung,* thus more for its questions than for its answers. For the portions of *De rerum natura* devoted to cosmogony turn out to be a veritable checklist of the issues with which the subsequent history of philosophical speculation about the origins of the universe would have to deal, continuing even into the modern era, and to which therefore the counterpoint between the *Genesis* of Moses and the *Timaeus* of Plato in Alexandria, New Rome, and Catholic Rome would have to be addressed.

Logically the first such issue is the question of beginnings itself. Lucretius set it forth as his "opinion" that the world was characterized by "nouitas" and had not yet been in existence for very long.[16] About air, for example, he opined that it "never stops being produced" [haud cessat gigni], but also that it subsequently "falls back into things" [in res reccidere].[17] As that observation suggests, moreover, he frequently correlated the question of the beginning of the world with the question of its ending, "creation" with "eschatology," to use, anachronistically but almost irresistibly, the later language of Christian theology. To introduce the various components of his cosmogony (including, basically in this order, earth, sky, sea, stars, the sun and moon, the animals, and humanity), he took as his theme and "the order of his design" "how the world consists of a mortal body and also has been born" [ut mihi mortali consistere corpore mundum / natiuumque simul ratio reddunda sit esse].[18] His observation of how the "maxima mundi membra" were subject to the process of being "consumpta [et] regigni" convinced him "that heaven and earth also once had their time of beginning and will have their destruction in the future" [caeli quoque item terraeque fuisse / principiale aliquod tempus cladem-que futuram].[19] But beyond that, the specifics of both creation and escha-

---

15. Lucr. 5.335–37. As Leonard and Smith (1942, 674) suggest, this claim was not altogether sound, for Cicero had already treated Epicureanism in prose, though not in poetry.

16. Lucr. 5.330–31.

17. Lucr. 5.279–80.

18. Lucr. 5.64–66.

19. Lucr. 5.243–46.

tology were, he added, unanswerable questions, what the "mundi geni-talis origo" had been and likewise what its "finis" would be.[20]

Philosophy and Traditional Religion

Because the cosmogonic myth has been one of the most universal in the history of religion, scientific investigation of cosmic origins and philo-sophical reflection about them must come to terms with the question of what to do about myth, as the bitter debates over creationism in the nineteenth and twentieth centuries have amply demonstrated. "Once upon a time, so the story goes" [semel, ut fama est] was the formula by which Lucretius dealt with the myth of the flood,[21] which soon thereafter was to be retold for Roman readers by Ovid.[22] The reservations and the distancing expressed in that formula applied to his treatment of other myths, as well as to his handling of traditional religious rituals or "sollem-nia sacra."[23] Thus, paraphrasing and summarizing the myth of Phaëthon, which was likewise a subject in Ovid's narrative, and which had figured in the narrative of Plato's *Timaeus* as well,[24] he identified it as "the tale which the old Greek poets have sung"; but having done so, he rendered the judgment that "this is all removed by a great distance from true reasoning," [quod procul a uera nimis est ratione repulsum],[25] because, as the Lucretian theology has been summarized, for him "there is no ever-lasting sun, no *pater omnipotens* (399), and indeed no Phaëthon."[26] In keeping with that theology, his explanation of the origins of "religio" (a term that has been rendered into English by more than one translator as "superstition" rather than as "religion") was based on both subjective and objective grounds. Subjectively, it took its rise, he suggested, from the manifestation, in the world of dreams, of beings who were beautiful in appearance and superhuman in stature, to whom humanity an-thropopathically attributed such qualities as sensation, everlasting life, and eternal beatitude, thereby elevating to the realm of a supposed super-natural reality what were in fact the fleeting illusions of the moment.[27] The objective grounds are more relevant here; for it was to the primitive

20. Lucr. 5.1211–13.
21. Lucr. 5.395, 412.
22. Ov. *Met.* 1.262–347.
23. Lucr. 5.1163.
24. Ov. *Met.* 1.750–2.400; Pl. *Ti.* 22C.
25. Lucr. 5.396–410.
26. Rouse and Smith 1992, 409.
27. Lucr. 5.1169–82.

discovery that the rotation of the heavens and the changing of the seasons took place "ordine certo," but to the impossibility nevertheless of discovering the ultimate causes of these observed phenomena, that Lucretius ascribed the almost incurable human tendency "omnia diuis tradere" and the almost ineradicable human belief that it was the gods who governed the universe.[28] And because, despite all the "ordo," the realm of nature was frequently punctuated by violent interruptions and eruptions, such as "threatening thunderstorms" [murmura magna minarum], these events were thought to be a deliberate expression of the will and the "bitter wrath" of the gods. "O miseras hominum mentes, o pectora caeca!" and "O genus infelix humanum!"[29] was the only appropriate response to such a predicament.

Although religion looked to the intervention of the gods for deliverance, the deliverance of the unfortunate human race from this blindness and superstition and the discovery of true reasoning, both philosophically about "religio" and scientifically about the universe, had actually been the accomplishment of a "Graius homo," Epicurus, "the ornament of the Greek nation" [Graiae gentis decus].[30] Lucretius even exclaimed of him, "He was a god, a god he was" [deus ille fuit, deus], so that it is no exaggeration to speak somewhat paradoxically of "the deification of Epicurus" in Lucretius.[31] At the beginning of his poetic-scientific treatise, Lucretius hailed Epicurus as one who, refusing to be intimidated by the "fama deum" or by the power of the elements, "ranged over the immeasurable universe with his mind and imagination" [omne immensum peragrauit mente animoque]. The "victory" he won by this intellectual and imaginative boldness was to achieve, for the first time ever, a sound cosmogony that was free of superstition, the profound and brilliant insight into "what has the possibility of coming into being and what has not" [quid possit oriri, / quid nequeat].[32] At the center of that Epicurean cosmogony was a redefinition of divine agency, the recognition, which Lucretius voiced in book 2 and repeated almost verbatim in book 5, that "by no means has the nature of the universe been created for us by divine agency" [nequaquam nobis diuinitus esse creatam / naturam mundi].[33] The pious practice of heaping vow upon vow and sacrifice upon sacrifice

---

28. See Gale 1994, 85–94.
29. Lucr. 2.14, 5.1183–95.
30. Lucr. 1.66, 3.3.
31. Lucr. 5.8; Gale 1994, 191–207.
32. Lucr. 1.62–79.
33. Lucr. 2.177–81, 5.195–99.

came from that erroneous conception of divine agency, and then it fed that error in turn; for in human beings "the ability to contemplate the universe with a serene mind" [placata posse omnia mente tueri][34] corresponded to the recognition that the gods themselves were doing precisely that, being "placida cum pace quietos," and therefore were not constantly meddling in human affairs and cosmic laws, as myth and superstition had imagined them to be doing.[35]

From this recognition that the nature of the universe had not by any means been created by divine agency there logically flowed at least two philosophical conclusions with far-reaching consequences for the subsequent history of cosmogony, one of them chiefly literary and the other primarily theological. The first was the designation of "poetry" [carmen] as the fitting form for a cosmogony to take in attempting to give an account that would be "appropriate to the majesty of the universe" [pro rerum maiestate], because prose truly was not prosaic to do the job right.[36] This insight made the careful investigation and precise clarification of creation narrative as a distinct literary genre, as well as the specification of the kinds of truth claims (if any) that could legitimately be made for myth and those that could be made for poetry, a necessary part of any attempt to make responsible scientific and philosophical sense out of what had happened "in the beginning." And when the creation narratives under consideration were such masterpieces of literature—and, at least in some sense, of poetry—as *Genesis* and *Timaeus,* it would be unavoidable for the interpreter of either text, and a fortiori for an interpreter undertaking a comparison of the two texts, that the status of an account of creation as, in the words of *Timaeus,* no more than "a likely story" [ὁ εἰκὼς μῦθος][37] would require sound analysis and precise exegesis.

The second implication of Lucretius's thesis that the universe had not been created by divine agency was negative theology, a radical apophaticism about religious language, even (or especially) about language purporting to give an account of how the nature of the universe has been created by divine agency. Not only creation stories but all the mythopoeic theories, which "have located the dwellings and temples of the gods in heaven" [in caeloque deum sedes et templa locarunt],[38] needed to be

---

34. Lucr. 5.1198–1203.
35. Lucr. 6.68–79.
36. Lucr. 5.1–2.
37. Pl. *Ti.* 29D.
38. Lucr. 5.1188.

subjected to the drastic criticism of the "via negativa." It was literally quite incredible, "beyond your ability to believe, that the holy dwellings of the gods are situated in some parts of the universe" [non est ut possis credere, sedes / esse deum sanctas in mundi partibus ullis], in temples or groves or even in the heavens.[39] Nor was space the only category of metaphorical language that Lucretius subjected to this devastating apophatic critique: body, emotion, and the other attributes employed in the conventional mythological language of Greece and Rome about the gods all had to be interpreted negatively. He repeatedly insisted, in response to his critics, that his intention was not to abolish belief in the existence of the divine but to help his readers to put aside "thoughts that are unworthy of the gods and alien to their peace" [dis indigna putare alienaque pacis eorum]. In that campaign he rejected whatever contradicted the image of the gods as serene and tranquil, "placida cum pace quietos," which included all the wildly anthropomorphic and anthropopathic language of the classical myths.[40]

Heaven and Earth

It is a locution so widespread in literature and religion as to seem well-nigh universal to designate the whole of things as "heaven and earth," as, for example, *Genesis* does in its opening verse. The first two items in the list of things that Lucretius attributed to the functioning of a "coming together of matter" [congressus materiai] were "earth" [terra] and "heaven" [caelum], with "sky and sea, sun and moon" as, in one sense perhaps, belonging to one or the other of these two.[41] But even more basic than the distinction of these latter from "heaven and earth" was the distinction between "heaven" and "earth," and the question of how, in the words of *Genesis*, "God [or whosoever] divided the heaven from the earth." As the divider between the two, according to *Genesis*, God had set a רָקִיעַ, a "dome," a Hebrew term that the Septuagint translated as στερέωμα and the Vulgate as "firmamentum."[42] Lucretius, while rejecting the superstition of a divine agency in creation, was nevertheless obliged to speak, as *Genesis* had, about the act of dividing heaven and earth, "a terris altum secernere caelum,"[43] and as Ovid did about how "God—or kind-

---

39. Lucr. 5.146–47.
40. Lucr. 6.68–79.
41. Lucr. 5.67–69.
42. *Gn.* 1:6–8.
43. Lucr. 5.446.

lier Nature—rent asunder land from sky" [deus et melior litem natura . . .
caelo terras . . . abscidit].[44]

In some ways, even more fundamental to any cosmogony was the
question of the elements, the stuff from which the universe was made.
Ever since the pre-Socratics, that question had been bound up with the
scientific investigation of the four basic elements, which Plato seems to
have been the first to call στοιχεῖα, but which under the designation
ῥιζώματα had been identified already by Empedocles as earth, air, fire, and
water.[45] Lucretius was apparently the first to render στοιχεῖα with the
Latin *elementa*, both in the sense of "the ABCs" that still survives in the
English term *elementary school* and in the scientific and philosophical
sense derived from it, as in the English chemical term *table of elements*;[46]
the Greek vocable, too, carried both meanings. It was in the first of these
senses that the word was being used when he said that "elements [are
common to] words," but even in that context this point was being made to
illustrate the axiom that nothing could exist without "principia."[47] *Principium* was a translation for the Greek ἀρχή, a term that was common to
Timaeus and the Septuagint *Genesis* (and subsequently to the New Testament as well), so that *elementa* may already in this passage have some of
its more scientific and philosophical connotations. Those connotations
were the subject matter of a lengthy disquisition in book 1 of *De rerum
natura*.[48] The principal Latin technical term for the four elements employed in this disquisition was *primordia*: Lucretius criticized those who
"define the 'primordia' of things as soft,"[49] asserted that "the 'primordia'
ought to exhibit a nature that is secret and unseen,"[50] and argued against
the theory of the four elements on the grounds that "many 'primordia'
that are common to many things in many ways are mixed together in
things."[51] But this discussion concluded with a return to the term *elementa*, in which the two senses of the word illuminated each other:

All through these very lines of mine you see many "elementa" common to many words, although you must confess that lines and

---

44. Ov. *Met.* 1.21–22; see also the comments of Bömer 1969, 24.
45. See Claghorn 1954, 20–38.
46. *TLL* s.v. "Elementum."
47. Lucr. 1.196–98.
48. Lucr. 1.705–829.
49. Lucr. 1.753–54.
50. Lucr. 1.778–79.
51. Lucr. 1.814–16.

words differ one from another both in meaning and in the sound of their soundings. So much can "elementa" do, when nothing is changed but order; but those that are the "rerum primordia" bring with them more kinds of variety, from which all the various things can be produced.[52]

Considered discretely, each of the four elements of fire, air, water, and earth had served one or another natural philosopher as the explanation for the basic stuff of the universe; sometimes two of them had been linked, air with fire or earth with water; and sometimes, as in the cosmogonic theories of Empedocles, all four elements were fundamental. But all such theories "magno opere a uero longe derrasse uidentur" and "principiis tamen in rerum fecere ruinas."[53] Instead, Lucretius sought, for example, to explain fire naturalistically, as a result of lightning, rather than to make it the basic element.[54] Nevertheless, earth was for Lucretius in a unique category among the four, as the "universal mother" [omniparens] of all, including also fire, water, and air, "since it is from the earth that all things have been produced."[55]

Lucretius admitted that, although the theory of the four elements was an unacceptable oversimplification, it did make an accurate point by conceiving of the universe as cohesive, to which therefore the metaphor of the body could be applied: "All things consist of a body that is born and dies, and we must consider the nature of the whole world to be that way, too" [omnia natiuo ac mortali corpore constant, / debet eodem omnis mundi natura putari].[56] But in the cosmogony of Lucretius this familiar metaphor of "corpus" performed another critical function at the same time, that of documenting his materialism against one or another theory of soul. Setting forth the fundamental metaphysical presuppositions of his system, he posited a distinction between the two components of which the nature of the universe consisted: "corpora sunt et inane," physical objects and the void. The reality of the "corpora" as distinct entities was guaranteed by the testimony of "empirical sense-experience" [sensus] (which Greek philosophers, including Epicurus and Plato in *Timaeus,* together with his later Jewish and Christian disciples, called αἴσθησις, in contrast with νόησις, the reality apprehensible only to the mind), whose trust-

---

52. Lucr. 1.823–29.
53. Lucr. 1.705–41.
54. Lucr. 5.1091–93.
55. Lucr. 5.259, 795–96.
56. Lucr. 5.235–39.

worthiness was for Lucretius the basic epistemological assumption without which there could be no appeal to the judgment of "ratio" in any
philosophical and scientific inquiry "occultis de rebus." The "inane," or
void, was likewise an unavoidable presupposition, for it formed the
"locus ac spatium" within which these "corpora" were located and were
able to move about.[57] As an inclusionary metaphysic, the dualism of
"corpora" and "inane" thus provided a positive explanation of reality as
individual phenomena and as an entirety, but no less important for the
Epicureanism of Lucretius was its exclusionary function. "Praeterea nil
est," Lucretius asserted flatly: "Beyond these there is nothing that you
would be able to call distinct from all body and separate from the void, to
be identified as a nature that is a third in number."[58] There was no tertium
quid. From this exclusionary principle it necessarily followed that it was
"impossible for the nature of the mind [animi natura] to arise alone,
without the body," and from this in turn it further followed that "when
the body has come to its end, it is necessary to confess that the soul
[anima] has perished" as well.[59] For the inquiry into "what constitutes
the soul and the nature of the mind" [unde anima atque animi constet
natura] belonged right alongside the cosmogonic investigation "concerning things celestial" [superis de rebus],[60] and materialism went hand in
hand with the denial of the immortality of the soul.

But the Lucretian polemic against the doctrine of the four στοιχεῖα and
the Lucretian axiom "Praeterea nil est" were also a way of introducing
another issue of metaphysics that already was an important subject for
inquiry and that would become much more important when the cosmogony of *Timaeus* and the cosmogony of *Genesis* came into collision
and counterpoint: the question of "creatio ex nihilo." For the fundamental cosmogonic question of the stuff from which the universe was made
was at the same time the question of the very definition of the verb *creare*,
as Lucretius made clear when he raised, to refute it, the theory "quattuor
ex rebus si cuncta *creantur.*"[61] Thus he established to his own satisfaction
that it was no more logical to call the στοιχεῖα the "rerum primordia"
than it was to make the "res" themselves primary and to derive the elements from them. Without invoking the verb *creare* in this context, he

---

57. Lucr. 1.419–29.
58. Lucr. 1.430–32.
59. Lucr. 3.788–99, 5.132–43.
60. Lucr. 1.127–31.
61. Lucr. 1.763.

pressed the same logic to reject, as even more unacceptable and absurd than the theory that "quattuor ex rebus cuncta creantur," the theory that these "cuncta" could have been created "ex nihilo." Therefore these words, quoted earlier, stand almost as an epigraph near the beginning of the work: "Principium cuius hinc nobis exordia sumet, / nullam rem e nilo gigni diuinitus umquam" [The first principle of our study we will derive from this, that no thing is ever by divine agency produced out of nothing]. This was, though with the significant addition of the term *diuinitus*, a verbatim translation of the axiom of Epicurus: πρῶτον μὲν ὅτι οὐδὲν γίνεται ἐκ τοῦ μὴ ὄντος.[62] Again translating from Epicurus, Lucretius went on to argue that the very particularity of individual things precluded a "creatio ex nihilo"; for "si de nilo fierent," it would be possible to produce anything from anything, and all distinctive identity would be lost.[63] As this rejection of nothingness pertained to beginnings, so it applied to endings as well: "Nature resolves everything into its elements, but it does not reduce things to nothing" [quidque in sua corpora rursum / dissoluat natura neque ad nilum interimat res].[64]

Necessity versus Teleology

The history of cosmogonic speculation based on *Timaeus* (which, though it called itself "a discourse concerning the Universe, how it was created or haply is uncreate" [περὶ ... τοῦ παντός ... ἦ γέγονεν ἢ καὶ ἀγενές ἐστιν],[65] did not seem to need to assert such a theory of "creatio ex nihilo") demonstrated that this theory was by no means the only way to give centrality to the notion of divine teleology. The subsequent history of the interpretation of *Genesis* (which did not explicitly assert it either, but which was eventually taken, by some Jews and by all Christians, to call for it in order to make consistent sense)[66] would show that the divine "creatio ex nihilo" being rejected by Lucretius was a powerful way to teach teleology; for it ascribed to the divine Creator the sovereignty and freedom not only to call things into being out of nonbeing but to stamp on them a design, and thus (in Aristotelian language) to connect first cause with final cause, ἀρχή with τέλος.[67] Therefore William Ellery Leonard, in his edition

---

62. Lucr. 1.149–50; see also Rouse and Smith 1992, 15, on this passage.
63. Lucr. 1.159–60.
64. Lucr. 1.215–16.
65. Pl. *Ti.* 27B–C.
66. On the history of this, see May 1994.
67. Arist. *Ph.* 2.3.194b–195a.

of *De rerum natura,* called attention to "the Lucretian reiteration against teleology."[68] It does seem that Lucretius was directing his polemic also, or even chiefly, against this teleological consequence of creation when he argued not only that the universality of transiency throughout the universe reached all the way, to affect also the temples and the "simulacra" of the gods, but that despite the appeals being made by human prayers and sacrifices, "the holy divinity" [sanctum numen] itself was powerless "to push forward the boundaries of fate" [fati protollere finis] or to resist the overwhelming power of "the laws of nature" [naturae foedera].[69] The description of primitive chaos, as a foil for the description of the structured system that was taken to be evident in the universe, would be, in the interpretation both of *Timaeus* and of *Genesis,*[70] one of the most decisive and dramatic instruments for the promotion of the idea of teleology and design; it may have been this also for Ovid's description of how "God—or kindlier Nature [deus et melior litem natura]—composed this strife."[71] But Lucretius anticipated its force and sought to dull its effect. "Every kind of beginnings" [omne genus de principiis] he saw as "gathered together into a mass," in which there was neither sun nor star nor sea nor sky, but the chaos of "some sort of unusual storm" [noua tempestas quaedam].[72] Unlike *Genesis* and *Timaeus,* however, *De rerum natura* over and over refused to take what they had seen as the logical next step from the description of chaos, which was the notion that "by divine agency" [diuinitus] this chaos had been transformed into the order of creation,[73] when, in the words of *Timaeus,* the Creator "brought it into order out of disorder" [εἰς τάξιν . . . ἐκ τῆς ἀταξίας].[74]

The Lucretian rejection of divine agency as a means of accounting for the dissipation of chaos and the establishment of the order of creation reached its climax in two rhetorical questions that were to be, quite apart from Lucretius, of enormous importance for the further study of these issues, and thus also for the counterpoint between *Timaeus* and *Genesis:*

Whence was a pattern for making things [exemplum gignundis rebus] first implanted in the gods, or even a conception of humanity

---

68. Leonard and Smith 1942, 60.
69. Lucr. 5.305–10.
70. Pl. *Ti.* 30A, 52D–53C; *Gn.* 1:22.
71. Ov. *Met.* 1.7, 21.
72. Lucr. 5.432–37.
73. Lucr. 1.149–50, 2.177–81, 5.195–99.
74. Pl. *Ti.* 30A.

[notities hominum], so as to know what they wished to make and to see it in the mind's eye?

Or in what manner was the power of the first-beginnings [uis principiorum] ever known, and what they could do together by change of order, if nature herself did not provide a model for creation [specimen creandi]?[75]

There seems to be no definitive answer to the question of how much Lucretius may or may not have known about the previous history of the doctrine of creation as set down in *Timaeus* (which he could probably have read in Greek, but which had already been translated into Latin by Cicero) and in *Genesis* (which did already exist in Greek translation in his time among the Jews of the Diaspora).[76] But with such quasi-technical terms as *exemplum* and *specimen creandi,* he was, at least implicitly, challenging the Platonic belief in preexistent Forms and παραδείγματα on the basis of which the particular things of the empirical universe had been fashioned, together with the biblical belief, at any rate concerning the fashioning of humanity, that God made man in accordance with his own image and likeness. Even Ovid's suggestion of the possibility that "the god who made all else, designing a more perfect world, made man of his own divine substance" [siue hunc diuino semine fecit / ille opifex rerum, mundi melioris origo] came closer to *Timaeus* as well as also to *Genesis* than Lucretius did.[77] For to Lucretius Nature had immanently provided her own "model for creation," so that the "pattern for making things" was not to be attributed to divine agency of some sort, or of any sort, much less to what Ovid called "the providence of God" [cura dei], even if this phrase is taken as an "almost impersonal conception of the 'Creator of the world.'"[78]

To make this point, Lucretius took up the central issue of cosmogony: "In what ways that assemblage of matter established earth and sky and the ocean deeps, and the courses of sun and moon."[79] Even the grammar here carried philosophical connotations; for the subject of the predicate "established earth and sky" [fundarit terram et caelum] was not a single supreme God, as in the almost, but not quite, identical opening sentence of

---

75. Lucr. 5.181–86.

76. On the question of the sources known to Lucretius, see the bibliography of Johannes Mewaldt in *PW* s.v.

77. Ov. *Met.* 1.78–79; see the parallels cited in Bömer 1969, 43–44.

78. Ov. *Met.* 1.48; Bömer 1969, 33.

79. Lucr. 5.416–18, 67–69.

Genesis, nor an assemblage of lesser gods under the direction of a second-ary divine being or δημιουργός, as in the cosmogony of *Timaeus,* but the immanent and preexistent reality of "that assemblage of matter" [ille coniectus materiai] itself. When this assemblage of matter established earth and heaven, moreover, "it certainly was not by any design [consilio] of the first-beginnings that they placed themselves each in its own order with keen intelligence [sagaci mente]."[80] To the contrary, randomness ruled, with atoms moving together by chance and coming apart by acci-dent and "trying out all kinds of combinations, whatsoever they could produce by coming together" [omnia pertemptare, / quaecumque inter se possent congressa creare]. All of this had taken place not instantaneously, as the various myths of creation—Greek and Roman, or for that matter Jewish and Christian—seemed to teach, but "through a vast time" [per aeuom], until eventually "those come together which, being suddenly brought together, often become the beginnings of great things, of earth and sea and sky."[81] Here again, the language Lucretius chose was signifi-cant: these great things, such as earth and sea and sky, had come into being by processes that "often happen" [saepe fiunt], not as the harmonious conclusion of a grand design and purpose that was immanent in them, much less of one that was transcendent and that therefore was the free and contingent choice of God the Creator.

Just as the Latin word *principium* and its Greek counterpart ἀρχή could mean either "beginning" in the chronological sense, "first principle" in the epistemological sense, or "ground of being" in the metaphysical sense, so the dual meaning of the word *end,* chronologically as "conclusion" and metaphysically as "intention" or "purpose," which is visible also in the Greek τέλος, in the Latin *finis,* and in the familiar English distinction between "means" and "ends," has helped to shape the development of the teleological theory in cosmogony, by relating it to eschatology. Con-versely, the challenge of Lucretius to teleology faced the requirement of disengaging it from eschatology, so as to enable him to acknowledge that there would be an end-as-conclusion for the universe without being obliged to follow earlier natural philosophers by smuggling in the tele-ological assumption that there had likewise been, from its "prin-cipium-ἀρχή," an end-as-intention in it all along. As has been noted ear-lier, the idea "that the world is subject to death and also has been born"

---

80. Lucr. 5.419–20.
81. Lucr. 5.422–31; see the parallels from elsewhere in the work (from both book 1 and book 5) noted in Rouse and Smith 1992, 412–13.

[mortal(em) mundum natiuumque esse],[82] and therefore the prediction "that heaven and earth also once had their time of beginning and will have their destruction in the future,"[83] underlay his entire cosmogony. In imagery that sometimes almost seemed redolent of apocalypticism, he prophesied to his patron Mennius that the threefold structure of the natural universe, sea and earth and sky, this "mighty and complex system of the world, upheld through many years, shall crash into ruins" [multosque per annos / sustentata ruet moles et machina mundi], and that "within some short time you will see violent earthquakes arise and all things convulsed with shocks," as "the whole world can collapse borne down with a frightful-sounding crash." Also in apocalyptic-sounding language, he admitted that what eye had not seen and ear had not heard was difficult to communicate and even more difficult to believe, just as *Timaeus* had declared, in a famous passage, "To discover the Maker and Father of this Universe were a task indeed; and having discovered Him, to declare Him unto all men were a thing impossible."[84] In so doing, Lucretius could even speak, in unconscious anticipation of the language that would be used in Catholic Rome, about "the highway of faith leading straight to the human breast and the temples of the mind" [uia qua munita fidei / proxima fert humanum in pectus templaque mentis], but also about a "persuasion that comes by reason rather than by the experience of reality" [ratio potius quam res persuadeat ipsa].[85] Even the myths of flood (which Lucretius introduced with the skeptical formula "Once upon a time, so the story goes" [semel, ut fama est])[86] and of fire (which he rejected with the formula "This is all very far indeed removed from true reasoning" [quod procul a uera nimis est ratione repulsum]),[87] could serve him in supporting his case for an eschatology divorced from teleology; for anyone who believed these myths "has to admit that destruction will come to earth and sky" [fateare necessest / exitium quoque terrarum caelique futurum].[88]

Both the Lucretian skepticism about any religious superstition that was based on myth and the Lucretian polemic against any philosophical or scientific cosmogony that was based on teleology were aimed at the doleful consequences of these beliefs. The epigram "So potent was Supersti-

---

82. Lucr. 5.64–66.
83. Lucr. 5.243–46.
84. Pl. *Ti.* 28C.
85. Lucr. 5.91–109.
86. Lucr. 5.395, 412.
87. Lucr. 5.396–410.
88. Lucr. 5.338–44.

tion in persuading to evil deeds" [Tantum religio potuit suadere mal-
orum], which "Voltaire, an ardent admirer of Lucretius, believed . . .
would last as long as the world,"[89] applied ultimately to both superstition
and belief in teleology, perhaps because Lucretius seemed to interpret such
philosophical notions as teleology and design as a more sophisticated, in
reality more sophistic, version of religious superstition. Someone who had
been "overborne by the terrifying utterances of the priests" [uatum /
terriloquis uictus dictis] and by their threats of everlasting punishment
after death, threats that were based on the doctrine of the immortality of
the soul, would thereby be deprived of the "strength to defy the supersti-
tions and threatenings of the priests" [religionibus atque minis obsistere
uatum] and would become their victim and prisoner.[90] Similarly, it was
necessary to recognize "by what force pilot nature steers the courses of the
sun and the goings of the moon," to avoid the twin dangers either of
supposing that the heavenly bodies moved "libera sponte sua" or of accounting for their motions "aliqua diuom ratione." Otherwise the scientific recognition of "how each thing has limited power and a deep-set
boundary mark [terminus]" would be replaced by a teleological speculation about the purpose and design "especially of those transactions which
are perceived overhead in the regions of ether," and this could produce a
relapse into the ancient superstition about omnipotent beings.[91]

The Order of Creation

The theory of teleology and the argument from design, which are perhaps
best known through the "five ways" of proving the existence of God given
at the beginning of the *Summa Theologica* of Thomas Aquinas, were
based on the perception that creation displayed a certain order. Lucretius
believed in the existence of order, too, and spoke of "how the array of
heaven and the various seasons of the years keep turning in a certain
order" [caeli rationes ordine certo / et uaria annorum . . . tempora
uerti];[92] but he did not draw from it such conclusions as teleology and the
argument from design, because his explanation of the order of creation
was fundamentally different.

For one thing, as that quotation indicates, the term *ordo* could pertain
to the concept of time itself; and, as the subsequent history of the doctrine

89. Lucr. 1.101; Rouse and Smith 1992, 11 n. d.
90. Lucr. 1.102–27.
91. Lucr. 5.76–90.
92. Lucr. 5.1183–84.

of creation would show, the relation between the creation of the universe and the creation of time demanded attention, whether it had been addressed overtly in a particular cosmogony, as by *Timaeus,* or more obliquely, as by *Genesis.* In one respect it can be said that Lucretius subordinated creation to time with his emphasis on the universality of change. "The nature of the whole world" [mundi natura totius] was not an immutable reality beyond time and change, but rather "time changes the nature of the whole world." It did so because "one state of things must pass into another, and nothing remains as it was [nec manet ulla sui similis res]"; the only thing that did remain immutable was mutability, as "all things move, all are changed by nature and compelled to alter."[93] That universal law of change affected not only the individual members of a species, which was obvious, but entire species as well, which perished either because they were "unable by procreation to forge out the chain of posterity" or because, not having the means of self-defense with which such beasts as lions were endowed, "they could neither live by themselves at their own will" nor commend themselves to the human race for their protection.[94]

Augustine's analysis of the flow of time, which he insisted moved from the future into the past, rather than the other way around as common sense supposed, would define past, present, and future as all in the present—a time present of things past, a time present of things present, and a time present of things future.[95] But it was consistent with the nominalistic approach of Lucretius to all abstractions when he denied the reality of time per se, applying the concept instead to the empirical experience of specific and concrete events as they were perceived to be shaping themselves into the order of past, present, and future. "Time as such," he asserted, "does not exist, but from things themselves there comes the sense of what has been done in the past, then what thing is present with us, further what is to follow afterwards" [tempus item per se non est, sed rebus ab ipsis / consequitur sensus, transactum quid sit in aeuo, / tum quae res instet, quid porro deinde sequatur].[96] No phenomenon more clearly or more regularly exemplified this order of creation than the rotation of the seasons. "We see many things," Lucretius pointed out, "that take place at a fixed time [certo tempore] everywhere," such as the blossoming of trees

---

93. Lucr. 5.828–31.
94. Lucr. 5.855–77.
95. Aug. *Conf.* 11.20.26.
96. Lucr. 1.459–61.

in the spring and the beginnings of a beard in adolescent boys. All of these "with regular sequence [conseque] now come back in fixed order [ex ordine certo]."[97] Fixed time and the fixed order of events were lessons that were learned from the sun and moon, "those watchful sentinels" that, as they traveled across the "great rotating temple" of the sky, "taught men well that the seasons of the year [annorum tempora] come around, and that all is done on a fixed plan and in fixed order [certa ratione atque ordine certo]."[98]

The concept of "the order of creation" could refer as well to the sequence according to which the several ranks of creatures had put in their appearance. This sense of the term was to be a persistent theme of cosmogony, also as documented both in *Genesis* and in *Timaeus*, each of which paid attention to which species had followed which in coming into being. Thus Ovid, too, enumerated in their sequence the way stars, fish, beasts, and birds had been produced,[99] in order then to point out that "there was still lacking an animal more sacred [sanctius] than these, more capable of high intelligence, and more able to exercise rule over the others"; and therefore "natus homo est" or he was created through a divine seed by "ille opifex rerum."[100] Lucretius did not linger over quite the same catalog of species, at least partly because his primary interest was in asserting their common origin in the earth as the universal mother and thus in denying the traditional doctrine of the other three στοιχεῖα, namely, fire, air, and water. Lucretius did posit that the "many things" [multa] of the universe came into being "modis multis uaria ratione," but nevertheless that in all of these ways earth "created" [creauit] them all.[101] Therefore it followed "that the earth deserves the name that she possesses, mother, since it is from the earth that all things have been produced";[102] or, as he put it elsewhere, earth was "the universal mother" [omniparens] and "the common sepulcher."[103] Whatever their sequence may have been, moreover, it was clear that "in the beginning" [principio] the earth produced herbs and plants,[104] and that then "the race of winged things"

---

97. Lucr. 5.669–79.
98. Lucr. 5.1436–39.
99. Ov. *Met.* 1.73–75.
100. Ov. *Met.* 1.76–81.
101. Lucr. 5.790–94.
102. Lucr. 5.795–96.
103. Lucr. 5.258–60.
104. Lucr. 5.783–84.

[genus alituum] had come, also "in the beginning" [principio].[105] Finally, in an interesting parallel between Lucretius and the etymology of "Adam" in *Genesis,* had come the human race, likewise from the earth, but "hardier, as was fitting inasmuch as the hard earth had made it."[106] Thus despite their radical differences, both Lucretius and *Genesis* could have formulated the purpose of their cosmogonies in the words of the conclusion of *Timaeus,* "to give a description of the universe up to the production of the mankind" [περὶ τοῦ παντὸς μέχρι γενέσεως ἀνθρωπίνης].[107]

A consideration of the distinctiveness of the human race in comparison with other species led to the question of the origins of language, which included the naming of the other species—"in what manner the human race began to use variety of speech among themselves by means of the names of things" [quo modo genus humanum uariante loquella / coeperit inter se uesci per nomina rerum].[108] The repeated polemic of Lucretius against Platonic or other notions that the gods had created the world and had done so on the basis of some preexistent "Form" [notities] or "Pattern" [exemplum] (which Plato called παράδειγμα)[109] necessarily implied as its corollary that "it is a foolish notion" [desiperest] to imagine that the gods or anyone else had "distributed names among things and that from this source human beings had learned their first vocables."[110] For the origin of language was in fact quite the other way around: "It was nature that drove them to utter the various sounds of the tongue, and convenience that moulded the names for things" [uarios linguae sonitus natura subegit / mittere, et utilitas expressit nomina rerum].[111] Thus "natura" and even "utilitas" acquired the sovereign freedom of action in creation—almost, if not quite, with a mind of their own—that Lucretius refused to allow the gods or the preexistent Forms to possess in creating. But his rejection of the idea of a divine "exemplum" for language evidently did not preclude a process of patterning that had moved in the opposite direction. For "imitating with the mouth the liquid notes of the birds came long before men could delight their ears by trilling smooth melodies in song."[112] What was true of vocal music applied as well to instrumental

105. Lucr. 5.801–2.
106. Lucr. 5.925–26; cf. *Gn.* 2:7, 1 *Cor.* 15:47.
107. Pl. *Ti.* 90E.
108. Lucr. 5.71–72.
109. Lucr. 5.181–86; Pl. *Ti.* 29B.
110. Lucr. 5.1041–43.
111. Lucr. 5.1028–29.
112. Lucr. 5.1379–81.

music, for which "the zephyrs whistling through hollow reeds taught the countrymen to blow into hollow hemlock-stalks."[113]

Although the explanation in *Genesis* that "on the seventh day [God] rested" was connected causally there and elsewhere in the Hebrew Bible with the divine institution of the Sabbath,[114] it had a cosmogonic as well as a liturgical function. For despite later theological efforts to blur or even obliterate the traditional distinction between the doctrine of creation and the doctrine of preservation,[115] cosmogony did seem to require closure. Lucretius did not need to ground a religious observance such as the Sabbath, or even the cosmos, in a myth of divine action; on the contrary, he separated "sollemnia sacra"[116] from such myths. Nevertheless, he, too, could have said, as *Genesis* did, that "God ended his work [of creating],"[117] but with the important distinction, once again, that the subject of the sentence was not the one "God" of monotheism, or even the many "gods" of polytheism, but the Earth herself: "She herself created the human race. . . . But because she must have some limit to her bearing, she ceased" [genus ipsa creauit / humanum. . . . Sed quia finem aliquam pariendi debet habere, / destitit].[118]

As was pointed out at the beginning of this chapter, Lucretius was well aware of his pioneering position in Latin science, philosophy, and literature. He was no less aware, however, of the colonial status of Latin science, philosophy, and literature in relation to the Greeks. "Nor do I fail to understand," he explained almost apologetically in the introduction to his epic, in a topos that other writers of philosophical (and theological) Latin were to repeat for centuries to follow, "that it is difficult to make clear the obscure discoveries of the Greeks in Latin verses, especially since we have often to invent new words because of the poverty of the language and the novelty of the subjects" [Nec me animi fallit Graiorum obscura reperta / difficile inlustrare Latinis uersibus esse, / multa nouis uerbis praesertim cum sit agendum / propter egestatem linguae et rerum nouitatem].[119] In this tribute to the superiority of the Greeks, both philosophically and linguistically, he was thinking chiefly of Epicurus, that "Graius homo"

---

113. Lucr. 5.1382–83.
114. *Gn.* 2:3; *Ex.* 20:8–11.
115. On the distinction and the connection between them, cf. Henry Pinard in *DTC* s.v. "Création."
116. Lucr. 5.1163.
117. *Gn.* 2:2.
118. Lucr. 5.822–27.
119. Lucr. 1.136–39.

and "Graiae gentis decus,"[120] and of Epicurus's disciples. Eventually the Epicurean materialism of Lucretius was to be vindicated as in some ways an anticipation of the direction that would be taken by important lines of development in modern science, as Albert Einstein's brief but eloquent tribute to Lucretius made clear when he expressed his admiration for this "man who was gifted with scientific and speculative interest, amply supplied with vivid feeling and thought," and who was "firmly convinced, and indeed believed that he could prove, that everything depended on the regular movement of unchangeable atoms."[121] But in the meantime, for the next thousand years and more, the future of cosmogony did not in fact belong to Epicurean and Lucretian materialism, whether Greek or Latin. It belonged instead, in the Greek-speaking realms of Alexandria and New Rome and even in the Latin-speaking realm of the "imperium Romanum" and Catholic Rome, to the theistic nonmaterialism of two other pre-Roman—and, certainly from Lucretius's perspective, prescientific—cosmogonies, *Genesis* and *Timaeus*. But the questions of cosmogony as they had been formulated by Lucretius nevertheless continued to dominate the philosophical discussion of these creation stories.

---

120. Lucr. 3.3.
121. Einstein 1924, VIa.

II

Athens: *Geneseōs Archē* as "The Principle of Becoming" (*Timaeus* 29D–E)

As Lucretius acknowledged in his eloquent tributes to Epicurus, that "Graius homo" and "ornament of the Greek nation" [Graiae gentis decus],[1] it was from Athens that classical Rome learned to think philosophically about cosmogony, which thus became one of the most illustrious examples of the process described in the familiar words of Horace "Graecia capta ferum victorem cepit et artes / intulit agresti Latio" [Greece, the captive, made her savage victor captive, and brought the arts into rustic Latium].[2] And the Athenian cosmogony that became the teacher of Rome—first of classical Rome through its translation by Cicero, then of New Rome where it could be read in the original Greek, and then of Catholic Rome through its translations by Cicero and then by Calcidius and through its verse paraphrase by Boethius—was the *Timaeus* of Plato, which Paul Shorey, with a characteristic flourish, once called "Plato's discourse on creative evolution, his pre-Socratic prose poem, his hymn of the universe, his anticipatory defiance of the negative voice of Lucretius' *De rerum natura*."[3] *Timaeus* was, in the words of its most influential translator into English, Benjamin Jowett, "the greatest effort of the human mind to conceive the world as a whole which the genius of antiquity has bequeathed to us";[4] according to a more recent translator of *Timaeus* into English, Francis Cornford, Plato here "introduced, for the first time in Greek philosophy, the alternative scheme of creation by a divine artificer, according to which the world is like a work of art designed with a purpose."[5] It was the only dialogue of Plato known in anything near its entirety to the Latin Middle Ages, and therefore it has had the longest continuous influence of any of the dialogues in the West. "There

---

1. Lucr. 1.66, 3.3.
2. Hor. *Epist.* 2.1.156–57.
3. Shorey 1933, 332; see also Shorey 1938, 45.
4. Jowett 1953, 3:702.
5. Cornford 1957, 31.

was," Raymond Klibansky has said, "hardly a medieval library of any standing which had not a copy of Chalcidius' version and sometimes also a copy of the fragment translated by Cicero. Although these facts are well known, their significance for the history of ideas has perhaps not been sufficiently grasped by historians."[6] Thus *Timaeus* occupied a unique place among the philosophical classics, and it was "of the greatest importance for ancient cosmological renewal ideology" and its medieval heirs.[7] Conversely, as Arthur Lovejoy has said, commenting specifically on *Timaeus,* "there is scarcely any general contrast between the Platonic strain in European thought down to the late eighteenth century and the philosophy of more recent times which is more significant than [the abandonment of the Timaean teleology]."[8]

As the most important classical cosmogony, this cosmogony of Athens would, in Greek-speaking Jewish Alexandria and Christian New Rome and in Latin-speaking Catholic Rome, inevitably come into counterpoint with the most important nonclassical cosmogony, that of Jerusalem in *Genesis.* To quote again from Jowett:

> The influence which the *Timaeus* has exercised upon posterity is due partly to a misunderstanding. In the supposed depths of this dialogue the Neo-Platonists found hidden meanings and connexions with the Jewish and Christian Scriptures, and out of them they elicited doctrines quite at variance with the spirit of Plato. Believing that he was inspired by the Holy Ghost, or had received his wisdom from Moses, they seemed to find in his writings the Christian Trinity, the Word, the Church, the creation of the world in a Jewish sense, as they really found the personality of God or of mind, and the immortality of the soul.[9]

This book is devoted to the history of that "misunderstanding." For the last of the issues enumerated by Jowett, the immortality of the soul, it was, however, not chiefly the *Timaeus* but above all the major Platonic dialogue on the subject, the *Phaedo,* that influenced one of the major Christian dialogues on the subject, *On the Soul and the Resurrection,* narrated by Gregory of Nyssa as having been carried on by his sister Macrina; this formulation articulated and decisively shaped Christian thought in a way

---

6. Klibansky 1981, 28.
7. Ladner 1959, 10.
8. Lovejoy 1936, 47.
9. Jowett 1953, 3:631.

that harmonized the two subjects of Gregory's title, the immortal soul and the resurrection of the body, into a single doctrine.[10] But *Timaeus* had an even more massive status than *Phaedo*. *Timaeus* affected principally the doctrine of what Jowett calls "the creation of the world in a Jewish sense," making it "the primary task of a history of Platonism in antiquity to trace the process by which the divine craftsman of the Timaeus could be made to resemble the Creator-God of the revealed religions, and the Platonic myth be taken as the philosophical authority for the idea that the cause of the world is the will of God."[11]

For beneath and behind all the misunderstanding, *Genesis* and *Timaeus* nevertheless manifested what the severest of all critics of the "Hellenization of Christianity," the liberal Protestant historian of dogma Adolf von Harnack, acknowledged (in his most widely circulated book) to be, using the Goethean phraseology so typical of him, "elements of elective affinity" [wahlverwandte Elemente].[12] Among such elements of elective affinity as well as of contrast, moreover, Harnack went on specifically to identify "the idea of creation."[13] These two chapters will be devoted to those elements of elective affinity and to the corollary difficulties raised by a contrapuntal reading of the two accounts of creation—first of the concepts of creation, for which *Timaeus* largely dictated the terms; then of the components of the creation, for which the sequence of the six days in *Genesis* provides the outline. To begin at the beginning, since both books were about the beginning, the first sentence of part 2 of *Timaeus*[14] contained the words ἡ τοῦδε τοῦ κόσμου γένεσις . . . κατ' ἀρχάς,[15] and the first words of the first chapter of the first book of the Bible were, in the Septuagint, Γένεσις [or even, in the Codex Alexandrinus, Γένεσις κόσμου]. ἐν ἀρχῇ ἐποίησεν ὁ θεὸς τὸν οὐρανὸν καὶ τὴν γῆν.[16] As they stood, these two formulas could be interchanged without doing violence to either; even the variant of the title of *Genesis* in the Codex Alexandrinus, which some biblical purists might be inclined to dismiss as an unwar-

10. Apostolopoulos 1986 is a close examination of the relation between Gregory's dialogue and Plato's.

11. Klibansky 1981, 51–52; see also his plate 5, Raphael's portrait of Plato with *Timaeus* in the fresco, *The School of Athens*.

12. Harnack 1901, 126.

13. Harnack 1901, 143. See also Jaeger 1961, 66–67, for a catalog of affinities.

14. According to the division in Cornford 1957, in which part 1, "The Works of Reason," begins at 29D; part 2, "What Comes of Necessity," at 47E; and part 3, "The Co-Operation of Reason and Necessity," at 69A.

15. Pl. *Ti.* 48A.

16. *Gn.* 1:1.

ranted "Hellenizing" intrusion of the concept of κόσμος into the text of the Bible, was borne out by the opening words of the second chapter of *Genesis* in all manuscripts, Καὶ συνετελέσθησαν ὁ οὐρανὸς καὶ ἡ γῆ καὶ πᾶς ὁ κόσμος αὐτῶν.[17] Whether they came directly from *Timaeus* to the translators of the Septuagint or not, the words γένεσις, ἀρχή, and κόσμος, moreover, were (along with many others to be noted later) only three of the elements of elective affinity evident already in the Greek vocabularies of *Genesis* and of *Timaeus* that would be deserving of comparative study in their own right.[18]

The Authority of a Cosmogony

Despite these elements of elective affinity, the two cosmogonies differed fundamentally in the way they presented the authority of their truth claims and in the self-consciousness with which they did so. Near the beginning of *Timaeus* there appeared the story in which "Solon, the wisest of the Seven," visited Egypt and was accosted by an aged priest, who told him: "Solon, Solon, you Greeks are always children: there is not such a thing as an old Greek. . . . You are young in soul, every one of you. For therein you possess not a single belief that is ancient and derived from old tradition, nor yet one science that is hoary with age" [Νέοι ἐστέ . . . τὰς ψυχὰς πάντες. οὐδεμίαν γὰρ ἐν αὐταῖς ἔχετε δι' ἀρχαίαν ἀκοὴν παλαιὰν δόξαν οὐδὲ μάθημα χρόνῳ πολιὸν οὐδέν].[19] By a process of natural selection in reverse, natural calamities, such as floods, had repeatedly obliterated collective memory in Greece, leaving "none of you but the unlettered and uncultured," with the result that Greek genealogies, for example, were "little better than children's tales."[20] In Egypt, by contrast, there were the traditions contained "in our sacred writings" [ἐν τοῖς ἱεροῖς γράμμασιν], which were "the most ancient" [παλαιότατα].[21] In a debate it was possible to invoke their authority, because the Egyptians still possessed "the actual writings" [αὐτὰ τὰ γράμματα].[22] Critias spoke of his account, which Solon had heard during his Egyptian visit, as "a story derived from ancient tradition" [λόγον . . . ἐκ παλαιᾶς ἀκοῆς], and he went on to

---

17. *Gn.* 2:1.
18. Such a list would overlap considerably with the "Glossary of Greek Technical Terms from Sources Ancient and Modern" in Pelikan 1993, 327–33.
19. Pl. *Ti.* 22B; see Froidefond 1971, 285–90.
20. Pl. *Ti.* 23B.
21. Pl. *Ti.* 23E, 22E.
22. Pl. *Ti.* 24A.

describe the process by which that tradition had been transmitted from Solon to "our great-grandfather Dropides, and Dropides told our grandfather Critias, as the old man himself, in turn, related to us."[23] In this contrast as drawn by *Timaeus*, the cosmogony of *Genesis* would clearly have ranked itself not only as one of those traditions whose account of the creation was contained "in our sacred writings," which were "the most ancient," but as preeminent, indeed unique, among them. And the childhood of Moses in Egypt—which, it deserves to be noted, was seen as belonging to "Asia" (meaning Asia Minor), not to Africa (known here as "Libya")[24]—would become, for both Jewish and Christian interpreters, the explanation for his having received a royal education, in which he was "trained in all the wisdom of the Egyptians."[25]

According to the account being expounded by Timaeus the narrator, cosmogonic accounts belonged to these ancient traditions, but they had to be interpreted properly. As the foundational presuppositions for its description of origins, *Timaeus* posited, at the very beginning of its cosmogonic discourse, two closely related distinctions, which in one form or another were to recur throughout the subsequent history of its interpretation as well as of its interaction with *Genesis*. As the character Timaeus declared.

> First of all, we must, in my judgment, make the following distinction. What is that which is Existent [τί τὸ ὄν] always and has no Becoming? And what is that which is Becoming always and never is Existent? Now the one of these is apprehensible by thought with the aid of reasoning [νοήσει μετὰ λόγου περιληπτόν], since it is ever uniformly existent; whereas the other is an object of opinion with the aid of unreasoning sensation [δόξῃ μετ' αἰσθήσεως ἀλόγου], since it becomes and perishes and is never really existent.[26]

That was the familiar, and fundamental, Platonic distinction between two objects of knowledge: "what is perceptible to the senses" [τὸ αἰσθητόν], a term that *Timaeus* derived etymologically from the verb ἀίσσειν (to rush), because of the different "motions rushing through the body" by way of the senses;[27] and "what is apprehensible only to the mind" [τὸ νοητόν].

23. Pl. *Ti.* 20D–E.
24. Pl. *Ti.* 24B–E.
25. Phil. *V. Mos.* 1.20; *Ac.* 7:22.
26. Pl. *Ti.* 28A.
27. Pl. *Ti.* 43C.

This distinction defined, for example, the terms in which *Timaeus* treated the doctrine of the soul, which, "having come into existence by the agency of the best of things apprehensible only to the mind [τῶν νοητῶν] and ever-existing as the best of things generated," was able to "partake in reasoning and in harmony," but which was also able to form "opinions and beliefs which are firm and true" [δόξαι καὶ πίστεις βέβαιοι καὶ ἀληθεῖς], when it was concerned with "what is perceptible to the senses" [τὸ αἰσθητόν].[28]

As those words suggest, the second distinction was the one between Truth (ἀλήθεια) and mere Belief (πίστις). Sometimes, especially in its earlier sections, the dialogue operated with a conventional and common-sense form of that distinction. As already mentioned, the contrast in historical reliability between Egyptian and Greek genealogies was that the latter were to be dismissed as "little better than children's tales."[29] When introducing his story about Solon, Critias called on Socrates to "listen to a tale which, though passing strange, is yet wholly true" [παντάπασί ἀ-ληθοῦς].[30] Socrates agreed that "the fact that it is no invented fable but genuine history [τό τε μὴ πλασθέντα μῦθον ἀλλ' ἀληθινὸν λόγον] is all-important."[31] Citing the myth of Phaëthon, son of Helios—to which, as mentioned in chapter 1, Lucretius would later refer as a "tale which the old Greek poets have sung," but which he dismissed on the grounds that it was "removed by a great distance from true reasoning"[32]—Critias acknowledged that it "has the fashion of a legend" [μύθου σχῆμα ἔχον], but he then proceeded to identify "the truth of it" [τὸ δ' ἀληθές] neverthe-less.[33] Likewise the story of the flood "is reckoned to be most ancient; the truth being otherwise . . ." [παλαιότατα, τὸ δὲ ἀληθές . . .].[34]

But the specifically Platonic version of the distinction, as applied to stories about cosmic origins, consisted of assigning the possibility of Truth only to a discussion of Being (οὐσία) itself and therefore of relegating all questions of Becoming (γένεσις) to Belief. That general principle carried over to accounts of creation:

We must affirm that the accounts given will themselves be akin to the diverse objects which they serve to explain; those which deal

28. Pl. *Ti.* 36E–37B.
29. Pl. *Ti.* 23B.
30. Pl. *Ti.* 20D.
31. Pl. *Ti.* 26E.
32. Lucr. 5.396–410.
33. Pl. *Ti.* 22C.
34. Pl. *Ti.* 22E.

with what is abiding and firm and discernible by the aid of thought will be abiding and unshakable; . . . whereas the accounts of that which is copied after the likeness of that Model, and is itself a likeness, will be analogous thereto and possess [no more than] likelihood.

By definition, therefore, an account of creation could only be a "likely account" [ὁ εἰκώς μῦθος], because both the teller of the narrative and the listener were "but human creatures," sharing a nature whose limitations compelled them to be content with this and no more;[35] for the distinction clearly implied that Belief could never aspire to Truth, which dealt with "the principle of all things, or their principles" [ἀπάντων εἴτε ἀρχὴν εἴτε ἀρχάς], a topic on which "it is difficult to explain our views while keeping to our present method of exposition," the likely account.[36]

Developing these distinctions a little later, the dialogue correlated "the accurately true argument" [ὁ δι' ἀκριβείας ἀληθὴς λόγος] and "the really existent" [τὸ ὄντως ὄν].[37] Recapitulating the arguments of the *Republic* about the constitution of the πόλις before going on to discuss the constitution of the κόσμος,[38] *Timaeus* picked up its discussions where the *Republic* had left off, although that does not even nearly resolve the complex problem of its place in the chronological sequence of Plato's works.[39] In the plan of the dialogues, moreover, Critias was to follow the cosmology of his colleague Timaeus with another examination of the πόλις.[40] This second part of the proposed trilogy, the *Critias*, survives only in a fragment, perhaps because its proposed topic was taken up by Plato's *Laws* instead and at great length; and the third part, *Hermocrates*, does not survive at all and probably was never composed. It would therefore appear to be legitimate to take this literary and philosophical connection between the *Republic* and *Timaeus*, and between *Timaeus* and the aborted *Critias*, as a ground for applying to the myth of cosmogony the more general epistemological strictures of the myth of the cave in book 7 of the *Republic*. Narratives of Becoming (γένεσις), then, had to be seen as "shadows" on the wall of the cave.[41] Also according to *Timaeus*, Being

---

35. Pl. *Ti.* 29B–D.
36. Pl. *Ti.* 48C.
37. Pl. *Ti.* 52C. On "Real Being," see the summary comments of Mohr 1985, 49–52.
38. Pl. *Ti.* 17C–19B. See Hirsch 1971, 337–85, esp. 363–65.
39. Raeder 1905, 374–94; Sayre 1983, 238–67; Burnet 1928, 51, 83.
40. Pl. *Ti.* 27B–C.
41. Pl. *Resp.* 7.514A–517A.

was accessible only to νοῦς as understanding, not to δόξα as opinion or belief, much less to αἴσθησις as sense perception.[42] As it was applied to cosmogony, it was the intent of this distinction to "preserve the probable account" [τὸν εἰκότα λόγον διασῴζειν].[43] Within those limits, then, it was possible even in setting forth a cosmogony to "be reasonably well provided for the task of furnishing a satisfactory discourse [λόγον τινὰ πρέποντα]—which in all such cases is the greatest task."[44] As G.E.R. Lloyd has said, this "reluctance to claim any more than a certain probability is readily understandable, indeed laudable when we reflect on the excessive dogmatism shown in this general area of inquiry not only by most of Plato's predecessors but also by most of his successors."[45]

Nevertheless, in the course of developing these distinctions and applying them to creation narratives, *Timaeus* did go on in several passages to raise the question of authority, even of divine authority (though not specifically of "sacred writings"), in a form that established connections or counterpoint both with the polemics of the *De rerum natura* of Lucretius and with the truth claims of the *Genesis* of Moses. It did so, however, almost tangentially, because several of these references seem to be spoken with what have been called "chuckles of play and irony in Timaeus' voice."[46] The most clearly ironic of these passages was the description of "the gift of divination" [μαντική] and of "the tribe of prophets" [τὸ τῶν προφητῶν γένος], who functioned as "prophets of things divined" [προφῆται μαντευομένων].[47] The most important of these passages, certainly for the subsequent development of that counterpoint and probably also for the argument of the dialogue itself, was its most specific reference anywhere to the radical apophaticism about religious language described in chapter 1. Timaeus, as part of his "prelude" [προοίμιον] as Socrates called it,[48] warned Socrates and his other hearers, "To discover the Maker and Father of this Universe were a task indeed; and having discovered Him, to declare Him unto all men were a thing impossible" [τὸν μὲν οὖν ποιητὴν καὶ πατέρα τοῦδε τοῦ παντὸς εὑρεῖν τε ἔργον καὶ εὑρόντα εἰς πάντας ἀδύνατον λέγειν].[49] This warning, which, as Henry Chadwick has

---

42. Pl. *Ti.* 51D–E.
43. Pl. *Ti.* 56A; Gloy 1986, 33–43.
44. Pl. *Ti.* 26A.
45. Lloyd 1983, 22.
46. Alexander P.D. Mourelatos in Bowen 1991, 29.
47. Pl. *Ti.* 71E–72B.
48. Pl. *Ti.* 29D.
49. Pl. *Ti.* 28C.

pointed out, went on to become "perhaps the most hackneyed quotation from Plato in Hellenistic writers,"[50] divided the issue into its two constituent parts, which were closely related but not identical: discovering "the Maker and Father of this Universe," whether through investigation or revelation, which it identified as "a task [ἔργον] indeed," but presumably an attainable one, inasmuch as the balance of the dialogue was devoted to it; and then declaring "Him unto all men," which, despite the apparent attempt of Timaeus in the dialogue to be doing precisely that, it called "impossible" [ἀδύνατον], at least partly because of the tendency of human language, like the rest of human existence, to "partake of the accidental and casual" [μετέχειν τοῦ προστυχόντος τε καὶ εἰκῇ].[51]

Some of what this important passage may be seen as implying was suggested at two later places. Directly after the correlation just cited between "the accurately true argument" and "the really existent,"[52] the dialogue turned to the στοιχεῖα (though without calling them that) of fire, earth, water, and air, and to the question of their "principles" [ἀρχαί]. The explanation of these principles, as the reader of Timaeus should by now expect to be warned, was necessarily restricted to "a method in which the probable is combined with the necessary" [κατὰ τὸν μετ' ἀνάγκης εἰκότα λόγον]. But the warning did not leave it at that. Rather, the discourse proceeded to add, "The principles which are still higher than these are known only to God and to the man who is dear to God" [τὰς δ' ἔτι τούτων ἀρχὰς ἄνωθεν θεὸς οἶδε καὶ ἀνδρῶν ὃς ἂν ἐκείνῳ φίλος ᾖ].[53] Turning later to the nature and origin of the soul, the dialogue invoked yet once more the familiar distinction between "the Truth" [τὸ ἀληθές] and "the likely account" [τὸ εἰκός]. But once again the distinction was qualified in a significant and even portentous fashion: "Only if God concurred [θεοῦ ξυμφήσαντος] could we dare to affirm that our account is true"[54]—a possibility that, despite the references to "divine inspiration" [ἐνθουσιασμός] and to "divination" [τὸ μαντεῖον],[55] was obviously beyond human powers.

Thus what the Timaeus left problematic—the concept of a knowledge about the Maker and Father of this Universe that only God and those dear to God could possess, and then only on the condition of divine

---

50. Chadwick 1953, 429 n. 1. See also Shorey 1938, 74, 79, 80; Nock 1962.
51. Pl. Ti. 34C.
52. Pl. Ti. 52C.
53. Pl. Ti. 53D.
54. Pl. Ti. 72D.
55. Pl. Ti. 71E.

concurrence—is what *Genesis* seems to have taken for granted; and what *Timaeus* took for granted—the distinction between Truth about Being and at best "a likely account" about Becoming—is what *Genesis* seems to have ignored. Its repeated refrain, "And God said" [καὶ εἶπεν ὁ θεός], was in the first instance a way of ascribing creative power to the absolute authority of the speaking and the word of God.[56] This contrasted with the emphasis of *Timaeus* on "Necessity yielding to intelligent persuasion" [δι' ἀνάγκης ἡττωμένης ὑπὸ πειθοῦς ἔμφρονος].[57] But it was also, in its almost matter-of-fact repetition, the ascription of a divine authority to the account itself as the word of God, the word of God that had come to Moses and was now coming through Moses. It does not seem to be an unwarranted conclusion to suggest from its very way of narrating the creation, as well as from its place within the context of the Hebrew Scriptures and of the faith of Israel, that for *Genesis* Plato's distinction in *Timaeus* between Truth and Belief was an utterly alien way of thinking and speaking.

Philosophy and Traditional Religion

Behind this difference between *Genesis* and *Timaeus* was an even more profound and fundamental one. To the writer and the intended readers of *Genesis,* the reality of God, of the one God confessed in the Shema, the liturgical formula of *Deuteronomy* 6:4, "Hear, O Israel, the Lord is our God, one Lord," was the nonnegotiable presupposition for any consideration of creation—or of anything else. That formula invoked the two most important names for God in the Hebrew Bible: יְהֹוָ֫ה [Yahweh], the tetragrammaton; and אֱלֹהִים. The first of these, at some point in the history of Judaism, came to be regarded as too sacred to be spoken, lest it be taken in vain,[58] and therefore it was pronounced as אֲדֹנָי (leaving the consonants intact in the text but adding substitute vowel points, which then produced, in various translations, the hybrid name *Jehovah*). The sacred name was therefore translated in the Septuagint as ὁ κύριος, as it was rendered also in the Greek of the New Testament. אֱלֹהִים, though a plural grammatically, was treated strictly as a singular in most passages of the Hebrew Bible. One of the exceptions to this was the declaration of the psalm, "You are gods, sons all of you of the Most High,"[59] which had the plural both in the Hebrew original and in the Greek and Latin transla-

---

56. Dürr 1938.
57. Pl. *Ti.* 48A.
58. Cf. *Ex.* 20:7.
59. *Ps.* 82:6 (NEB var.).

tions; it had, moreover, been quoted in the plural by Christ himself, and
with the added reinforcement that "Scripture cannot be set aside."[60] An
even more notable plural occurred in the biblical creation story, in the
sentence "Let *us* make man in *our* image and likeness."[61] In rendering the
Hebrew term, the Septuagint translators regularly employed the Greek
title ὁ θεός, despite its pagan provenance, though of course in the singular.
The Shema had equated the two titles and had neutralized the grammatical plural in the name אֱלֹהִים by declaring that the God so denominated
was nevertheless "one." The title אֱלֹהִים was employed throughout the
first of the two creation narratives in *Genesis*, now labeled as chapter 1 of
the book, while in the second creation narrative יְהוָה did the creating. It
has become a convention of the modern literary and historical-critical
study of *Genesis* to treat the two creation narratives as originally separate
sources, distinguished from each other by the use of the divine name, and
therefore usually identified, respectively, as "E" (or the "priestly account") and "J."[62] Whatever the validity and importance of that
historical-critical interpretation may or may not be as a literary hypoth-
esis, it is relatively unimportant in the present context. For all the interpreters with whom we are dealing here, both Jewish and Christian, treated
the equation of the two titles by the Shema as normative and therefore
treated the two creation narratives as part of one divinely inspired account, even though, as we shall see in chapter 4, Philo did take exegetical
advantage of the dual account in several important ways. Coincidentally,
the narrative of creation in *Timaeus* also told its story twice, so that the
Jewish and Christian interpreters of *Genesis* could have made their own
the formula at the midpoint of *Timaeus:* "At the commencement of our
account, we must call upon God the Saviour to bring us safe through a
novel and unwonted exposition to a conclusion based on likelihood, and
thus begin our account once more."[63]

As we shall see in later chapters, the use of the Hebrew plural in the
priestly creation narrative of *Genesis* could be a source of some embarrassment to both Jewish and Christian monotheism. But the latter turned
this embarrassment to its own advantage by interpreting that plural as the
first biblical reference to the doctrine of the Trinity; and at least in the
Latin Christianity of Augustine, the repetition of that plural in both the

---

60. *Jn.* 10:34–35.
61. *Gn.* 1:26.
62. Anderson 1977; Steck 1981.
63. Pl. *Ti.* 48D–E.

verb and the adjective of *Genesis* 1:26, "Faciamus hominem ad imaginem nostram," became the occasion for the Western Christian teaching that human nature, being the image not only of the oneness of the Godhead but of the Trinity, itself manifested a Trinitarian structure. None of that took anything away from the status of monotheistic worship as the most basic a priori of all in the biblical doctrine of creation, for Christians no less than for Jews. Without developing any speculative counterpart to the Platonic version of God as ὁ ὤν, the Hebrew Bible had made all being dependent on the reality of God; but in an act of linguistic boldness, the translators of the Septuagint produced "a nonphilosophical statement which has since become an epoch-making statement in the history of philosophy,"[64] when they rendered the divine explanation of the divine name to Moses at the burning bush, as recorded in *Exodus* 3:14, with the Greek formula !Εγώ εἰμι ὁ ὤν. That statement also helped to set the terms for the counterpoint between *Genesis* and *Timaeus* and made a consideration of this biblical a priori mandatory.

The relation of *Timaeus* to traditional Greek religion—what Harry Wolfson on the basis of *Timaeus* referred to as the Greek contrast between "an anti-mythological theism, in which God is conceived of as an artisan, and a mythological theism, in which God is conceived of as a begetter"[65]—is ambiguous, as two references to that tradition make clear. Near the outset of the dialogue, Critias introduces his story "both as a payment of our debt of thanks to [Socrates] and also as a tribute of praise, chanted as it were duly and truly, in honour of the Goddess [Athena] on this her day of Festival."[66] In response, Socrates describes it as "admirably suited to the festival of the Goddess which is now being held, because of its connexion with her."[67] A little later Socrates calls on Timaeus, the chief interlocutor from whom the dialogue takes its name, to speak "when you have duly invoked the gods" [καλέσαντα κατὰ νόμον θεούς] (the passage could also be translated: "when you have invoked the gods in accordance with the law"). The response of Timaeus to this specific request deserves to be quoted in full:

> Nay, as to that, Socrates, all men who possess even a share of good sense call upon God [θεὸν καλοῦσιν] always at the outset of every undertaking, be it small or great; we therefore who are purposing to

64. Gilson 1941, 40.
65. Wolfson 1956, 290.
66. Pl. *Ti.* 21A.
67. Pl. *Ti.* 26E.

deliver a discourse concerning the Universe, how it was created or haply is uncreate [περὶ . . . τοῦ παντός . . . ἢ γέγονεν ἢ καὶ ἀγενές ἐστιν], must needs invoke Gods and Goddesses [θεούς τε καὶ θεάς] (if so be that we are not utterly demented), praying that all we say may be approved by them in the first place, and secondly by ourselves.[68]

Quite apart from the question of the correlation between the plural θεοί in the request of Socrates and the singular θεός, followed by the plurals θεοί τε καὶ θεαί in the response of Timaeus, and of the oscillation between θεός, ὁ θεός, οἱ θεοί, and/or αἱ θεαί throughout the dialogue (of which more in a moment), the function of this speech of Timaeus may not have been easy to determine, even for ancient readers; but it "provided every commentator with a conventional occasion for his set piece on the subject of prayer"[69] In resuming the "probable account," Timaeus once more voiced the obligation to "call upon God the Saviour [θεὸν σωτῆρα] to bring us safe through a novel and unwonted exposition to a conclusion based on likelihood."[70] In any case, such statements appear to have been taken by Boethius, for example, as serious.[71]

The other explicit reference to the religious tradition was unmistakably ironic in its intent.[72] Any classical Greek cosmogony, including the cosmogony of *Timaeus*, was obliged to acknowledge that at least since the *Theogony* of Hesiod, cosmogony and theogony had been closely related in Greek thought. Therefore this passage contains by far the most detailed catalog in *Timaeus*—and together with the end of book 2 of the *Republic*,[73] one of the most detailed anywhere in the Platonic corpus—of the Homeric and Hesiodic gods: "Of Gê and Uranus were born the children Oceanus and Tethys; and of these, Phorkys, Cronos, Rhea, and all that go with them; and of Cronos and Rhea were born Zeus and Hera and all those who are, as we know, called their brethren; and of these again, other descendants." But that recitation of the traditional theogony of Olympus, which was scrupulously neutral in its tone and language, was set in the framework of an appeal to the authority of mythological tradition, which was in turn set in the framework of the fundamental epistemo-

---

68. Pl. *Ti.* 27B–C.
69. A.C. Lloyd in Armstrong 1967, 285.
70. Pl. *Ti.* 48D–E.
71. Boet. *Cons.* 3P9.32–33.
72. Pl. *Ti.* 40D–41A.
73. Pl. *Resp.* 2.377D–382C.

logical presupposition of the entire discourse. Thus the language of the preamble to the theogony was clearly ironic. "We must," Timaeus intoned, "trust to those who have declared it aforetime, they being, as they affirmed, descendants of gods [ἐκγόνοις μὲν θεῶν οὖσιν] and knowing well, no doubt, their own forefathers. It is, I say, impossible to disbelieve the children of gods." But this assertion was qualified by the introductory disclaimer that "to discover and declare their origin is too great a task for us"; the words "discover and declare" [εἰπεῖν καὶ γνῶναι]—Bury reverses the order in translation for the sake of logic—echoed the words of the earlier warning that "To discover the Maker and Father of this Universe were a task indeed; and having discovered Him, to declare Him unto all men were a thing impossible."[74] The assertion was further hemmed in by the stipulation that such traditional theogonies "lack either probable or necessary demonstration" [ἄνευ εἰκότων καὶ ἀναγκαίων ἀποδείξεων];[75] for the status of a "likely account" [ὁ εἰκὼς μῦθος] was as much as any account of "origin" [γένεσις], including Timaeus's own account, could be expected to attain,[76] while a "necessary" explanation had to be reserved to the Truth that dealt with Being rather than with Becoming. As various readers of *Timaeus,* above all Francis Cornford, have warned with considerable force, it must be noted that the dialogue did not make the "Creator-δημιουργός" the object of worship.[77] In this respect, therefore, although its doctrine of a divine creator put it on the same side as *Genesis* in opposition to *De rerum natura,* which denied divine agency in creation by its assertion "nequaquam nobis diuinitus esse creatam / naturam mundi,"[78] it was on the same side as the Lucretian account, and in opposition to *Genesis,* in that in effect cosmogony and liturgy were kept separate.

A plain recital and catalog (unencumbered for the present by commentary) of the God-language in the "treatment of a great host of matters regarding the Gods and the generation of the Universe" [περὶ θεῶν καὶ τῆς τοῦ παντὸς γενέσεως] by *Timaeus* will suggest why it would have to appear, as Timaeus warned Socrates, not "always in all respects self-consistent and perfectly exact"[79] to any reader, even to a Greek or Roman polytheist, but particularly to the Jewish and Christian monotheists who

74. Pl. *Ti.* 28C.
75. Pl. *Ti.* 40E.
76. Pl. *Ti.* 29D.
77. Cornford 1957, 34–35.
78. Lucr. 2.177–81, 5.195–99.
79. Pl. *Ti.* 29C.

would attempt to find its correlation with *Genesis*. Of the roughly seventy times in the entire dialogue when the word θεός or its cognates appeared in one form or another (including several passages already referred to), the singular θεός appeared by itself and without the article sixteen times;[80] ὁ θεός with the article and by itself likewise sixteen times;[81] ἡ θεός six times, all of them early in the dialogue;[82] θεός and ὁ θεός together three times, in the first of which θεός without the article was used twice;[83] θεοί without the article twenty times, one of these passages using it twice and another employing the form θεοὶ θεῶν;[84] οἱ θεοί with the article five times;[85] the adjective θεῖος, sometimes as a substantive, eleven times, two of these in one passage,[86] and the adjective θεοσεβέστατος once.[87] Other "divine" titles—apart from the seven instances of δημιουργός, to which we shall be returning[88]—included σωτήρ,[89] ποιητής,[90] and ὁ ποιῶν,[91] πατήρ,[92] ὁ τεκταινόμενος,[93] ὁ ἄριστος τῶν αἰτίων,[94] ὁ ξυνιστάς,[95] ὁ ξυνδήσας,[96] οἱ ξυστήσαντες,[97] δαίμων in reference to a god,[98] ὁ κηροπλάστης,[99] οἱ διακοσμοῦντες,[100] οἱ κρείττους,[101] τὸν τὰς ἐπωνυμίας θέμενον,[102] and οἱ μεταπλάττοντες.[103]

80. Pl. *Ti.* 21E, 27C, 44E, 46C, 47A, 48D, 53D, 68D, 71A, 71E, 72D, 80E, 90A, 92A, 92C.

81. Pl. *Ti.* 30A, 30C, 30D, 31B, 32B, 34C, 39B, 47C, 55C, 56C, 68E, 69B, 73B, 74D, 75C, 78B.

82. Pl. *Ti.* 21A, 23D, 24B, 24C, 24D, 26E.

83. Pl. *Ti.* 34A–B, 38C, 53B.

84. Pl. *Ti.* 24D, 27B, 27C, 29C, 39E, 40C, 40D (twice), 40E, 41A, 41C, 44D, 45A, 47C, 51E, 77A, 90D. Θεοὶ θεῶν is at 41A.

85. Pl. *Ti.* 22D, 37C, 40C, 42D, 45F

86. Pl. *Ti.* 40B, 41C, 44D, 68D, 68E (twice), 69C, 69D, 76B, 90A.

87. Pl. *Ti.* 41E.

88. Pl. *Ti.* 28A, 29A, 40C, 41A, 68E, 69C, 75B.

89. Pl. *Ti.* 22D, 48D.

90. Pl. *Ti.* 28C.

91. Pl. *Ti.* 31B, 76C.

92. Pl. *Ti.* 28C, 37C (ὁ γεννήσας πατήρ), 42E, 71D.

93. Pl. *Ti.* 28C.

94. Pl. *Ti.* 29A.

95. Pl. *Ti.* 29D, 30C, 32C, 36D.

96. Pl. *Ti.* 32C.

97. Pl. *Ti.* 71D.

98. Pl. *Ti.* 40D.

99. Pl. *Ti.* 74C.

100. Pl. *Ti.* 75D.

101. Pl. *Ti.* 77C.

102. Pl. *Ti.* 78E.

103. Pl. *Ti.* 92B.

As becomes evident from a comparison of the several standard translations of *Timaeus* into English—notably those of Benjamin Jowett, A.E. Taylor, Francis Cornford, and R.G. Bury—translators have striven to make consistent sense of this usage, especially of the singulars θεός and ὁ θεός: Jowett, and in considerable measure also Taylor, tended in the direction of at least as "monotheistic" a reading and rendering as the text would permit; Cornford, in reaction against them and especially against Taylor, avoided capitals, sometimes even substituted *Heaven* for *God,* and sought to screen out the influence of Judeo-Christian parallels, though some of them did creep in nevertheless; and Bury resolved the dilemma in the other direction, by capitalizing *Gods* as well as *God* most of the time.[104] Those differences among translators indicate that the questions are multiplied still further in English by the capitalization of the name *god/ God* and by the use of the definite article. In German all nouns are capitalized, and therefore the name is capitalized whether it refers to the one God of monotheism or to one of the several gods of polytheism, but in English capitalization is ordinarily an indication of monotheism. As subsequent chapters will suggest, the same philosophical issues underlying those problems of translation would, even absent the problem of capitalization, also vex subsequent interpreters of *Timaeus,* whether they were writing in the Greek in which the dialogue had been composed or in Latin, in which there was no article.

The Principle of Mediation

Whatever the language of the doctrine of God and of gods in *Timaeus* may have meant, the most intriguing figure in its cosmogony, and the most puzzling, was the divine agent of creation identified as ὁ δημιουργός. With the Demiurge there was introduced into the account of origins a divine principle of mediation as well as a counterforce of Reason (νοῦς, λόγος) to combat the workings of Necessity (ἀνάγκη), because "this Cosmos in its origin was generated as a compound, from the combination of Necessity and Reason" [ἡ τοῦδε τοῦ κόσμου γένεσις ἐξ ἀνάγκης τε καὶ νοῦ συστάσεως ἐγεννήθη].[105] As a consequence, two kinds of causes had to be distinguished, "the necessary and the divine" [τὸ μὲν ἀναγκαῖον, τὸ δὲ θεῖον], and the necessary causes had to be sought for the sake of the divine ones, because in the shaping of the cosmos, "the Artificer of the most

---

104. On the differences between Taylor and Cornford, see Des Places 1976, 21–23.
105. Pl. *Ti.* 48A.

beautiful and most good" [ὁ τοῦ καλλίστου τε καὶ ἀρίστου δημιουργός] had made use of things that were necessary as "subservient causes" [αἰτίαις ὑπηρετούσαις], for the sake of the Good, which was the primary cause.[106] In the strict sense, therefore, he was "the Constructor of things divine" [τῶν θείων δημιουργός] but not the author of "the structure of mortal things" [τῶν θνητῶν τὴν γένεσιν]. These latter were the work of the lesser gods whom the Demiurge created and to whom he entrusted this task. Thus the immortal soul came from the Demiurge, but the mortal body from the lesser gods.[107] Those works of which he was "Maker and Father" [δημιουργὸς πατήρ τε] were beyond the vicissitudes of Necessity and could be dissolved by his will alone.[108] The all-encompassing presupposition and conclusion regarding the creating action of the Demiurge came already near the beginning of the discourse: "If so be that this Cosmos is beautiful and its Constuctor good, it is plain that he fixed his gaze on the Eternal" [εἰ μὲν δὴ καλός ἐστιν ὅδε ὁ κόσμος ὅ τε δημιουργὸς ἀγαθός, δῆλον ὡς πρὸς τὸ ἀΐδιον ἔβλεπεν].[109] From this it followed that "for Him who is most good [τῷ ἀρίστῳ] it neither was nor is permissible to perform any action save what is most beautiful [τὸ κάλλιστον]."[110]

Because the all-encompassing presupposition of the creation narrative (or narratives) in *Genesis* was the monotheism spoken of earlier, there would seem to be no obvious way to make room in it for any divine principle of creative mediation corresponding to the Demiurge. Its opening sentence consisted of a prepositional phrase, ἐν ἀρχῇ, a transitive verb, ἐποίησεν, a single subject, ὁ θεός, and a direct object, τὸν οὐρανὸν καὶ τὴν γῆν, with neither an intermediary nor an instrument being specified.[111] But in the counterpoint with *Timaeus* there were at least two points of contact that went beyond this simplistic grammatical interpretation in making room also within the *Genesis* account for some parallel. One was the opening noun, ἀρχή, a term shared by the two cosmogonies as well as by the New Testament. For if the opening preposition, ἐν, which translated the Hebrew בְּ, were to be taken as "the ἐν of Accompanying Circumstances" characteristic of Septuagint Greek, which "includes the instrumental use, but goes far beyond it,"[112] then ἀρχή, with its many

106. Pl. *Ti.* 68E.
107. Pl. *Ti.* 69C.
108. Pl. *Ti.* 41A.
109. Pl. *Ti.* 29A.
110. Pl. *Ti.* 30A.
111. *Gn.* 1:1.
112. Conybeare and Stock 1988, 82–83.

different senses, especially in Christian Greek,[113] suggested, for example to Augustine, a possible analogue.[114] An even more attractive analogue was provided by the formula "And God said" [καὶ εἶπεν ὁ θεός], which occurred ten times in the first chapter. It made the speaking of God, whatever the metaphysical reality represented by this anthropomorphic metaphor was taken to be, the divine action in response to which one class of creatures after another came into being. Although this emphasis on the power of the word of God occupied a special place in the language and thought of the Hebrew Bible,[115] it could also be read as a reinforcement of some of the accents of *Timaeus*, despite its differences from the language of *Timaeus* about "Necessity yielding to intelligent persuasion" [δι᾽ ἀνάγκης ἡττωμένης ὑπὸ πειθοῦς ἔμφρονος].[116] When the cosmos was said to have been "constructed after the pattern of that which is apprehensible by reason and thought" [γεγενημένος πρὸς τὸ λόγῳ καὶ φρονήσει περιληπτόν],[117] the word λόγος, which would become a central element in the philosophical-theological vocabulary both of Alexandrian Judaism and of Christianity, could mean "reason" or "word" or both. An additional and more whimsical parallel to the creating force of the word of God in *Genesis* was provided by the comment of Critias about "mankind, already, as it were, created by [Timaeus's] speech" [ἀνθρώπους τῷ λόγῳ γεγονότας], referring to the discourse on creation that Timaeus was about to deliver in *Timaeus*, and then, in the *Critias*, to the one he had just delivered.[118]

Teleology versus Necessity

Genesis was seemingly altogether silent about two closely related questions on which the cosmogony of *Timaeus* and that of *De rerum natura* were in diametric opposition, both of them being questions that would be addressed to *Genesis* by readers who came to it from the reading of *Timaeus*: Why had the world been created? And according to what design and model had it been created? Both questions were ruled out of order by Lucretius, but both were central to *Timaeus*. Its answer to the first ques-

---

113. Lampe 234–36.

114. Aug. *Gen. Man.* 1.2.3.

115. So, for example, *Ps.* 33:6: τῷ λόγῳ τοῦ κυρίου οἱ οὐρανοὶ ἐστερεώθησαν καὶ τῷ πνεύματι τοῦ στόματος αὐτοῦ πᾶσα ἡ δύναμις αὐτῶν.

116. Pl. *Ti.* 48A.

117. Pl. *Ti.* 29A.

118. Pl. *Ti.* 27A; Pl. *Criti.* 106A.

tion was: "Let us now state the Cause wherefor He that constructed it constructed Becoming and the All. He was good, and in him that is good no envy [φθόνος] ariseth ever concerning anything; and being devoid of envy He desired that all should be, as far as possible, like unto Himself." That was, the discourse continued, "the supreme originating principle of Becoming and the Cosmos" [γενέσεως καὶ κόσμου . . . ἀρχὴν κυριωτά-την].[119] In relation to this "Form of the Most Good" [τὴν τοῦ ἀρίστου . . . ἰδέαν], all other "causes" in the cosmos were in fact only "auxiliary Causes" [ξυναιτίαι], even though "the most of men" thought of them as "primary causes."[120] The second question was, if anything, even more fundamental, as Lucretius knew when he asked his own two questions:

Whence was a pattern for making things [exemplum gignundis rebus] first implanted in the gods, or even a conception of humanity [notities hominum], so as to know what they wished to make and to see it in the mind's eye?

Or in what manner was the power of the first-beginnings [vis principiorum] ever known, and what they could do together by change of order, if nature herself did not provide a model for creation [specimen creandi]?[121]

For Lucretius, the answer was to deny the reality of any pattern or design at all.

But the answer of *Timaeus* was that this pattern for making things and model for creation (which it called παράδειγμα) was the design of which the cosmos was an image (which it called εἰκών).[122] It was unthinkable that this model or pattern should itself have belonged to the realm of those things that had not always been from eternity but had only come into existence. It was a general principle that "when the artificer of any object [ὁ δημιουργός], in forming its shape and quality, keeps his gaze fixed on that which is uniform, using a model of this kind, that object, executed in this way, must of necessity be beautiful [καλόν]."[123] That general principle was universally applicable to all making, including human creativity, but the supreme application of it was to the making of the universe, to cosmogony. From it, therefore, it ineluctably followed that "If so be that this

119. Pl. *Ti.* 29D–E; on the meaning of φθόνος, see Brisson 1974, 155 n. 1.

120. Pl. *Ti.* 46C–D.

121. Lucr. 5.181–86.

122. Pl. *Ti.* 29B.

123. Pl. *Ti.* 28A.

Cosmos is beautiful [καλός] and its Constructor good [ἀγαθός], it is plain that he fixed his gaze on the Eternal [πρὸς τὸ ἀίδιον]." Nothing else could have served as an appropriate παράδειγμα for a divine agent of creation who did not begrudge anything good but wanted to confer it.[124] Moreover, as was elaborated later in the dialogue, "all that is good is beautiful, and the beautiful is not void of due measure" [πᾶν δὴ τὸ ἀγαθὸν καλόν, τὸ δὲ καλὸν οὐκ ἄμετρον].[125]

This "due measure," or "proportionality" [ἀναλογία], gave harmony and unity to the universe: "The body of the Cosmos was harmonized by proportion and brought into existence. These conditions secured for it Amity [φιλίαν], so that being united in identity with itself it became indissoluble by any agent other than Him who had bound it together."[126] Although *Genesis* did not raise, much less answer, the question of why God had created the world, nor the question of its design and pattern, nor even the question of its harmony and unity, it did seem to be answering all three of these questions when it declared, decidedly and repeatedly, that the created world was, in the very same word employed by *Timaeus*, "beautiful" [καλός]: "And God saw that it was beautiful" [καὶ εἶδεν ὁ θεὸς τὸ φῶς ὅτι καλόν].[127] Indeed, the Septuagint even improved on the Hebrew original by adding it an extra time: καὶ εἶδεν ὁ θεὸς ὅτι καλόν.[128] And when *Genesis* in its summary of the six days said, "And God blessed them" [καὶ ηὐλόγησεν αὐτὰ ὁ θεός],[129] this seemed to be similar to the summary statement of *Timaeus* that "when the Father that engendered it perceived it in motion and alive, a thing of joy to the eternal gods, He too rejoiced"—provided that there could be a way to bend the phrase "the eternal gods" to the requirements of biblical monotheism, as eventually there proved to be both for Jewish and for Christian interpreters.[130] For if the Bible taught, here and elsewhere, that the created cosmos was καλός, and if it taught furthermore, not here but elsewhere, that God the Creator was ἀγαθός,[131] it might have to be called an extension or an expansion of the language of the Bible, but it could not be called a contradiction of it, to apply to the cosmogony of *Genesis* the formula from the cosmogony of

---

124. Pl. *Ti.* 29E.
125. Pl. *Ti.* 87C.
126. Pl. *Ti.* 32C.
127. *Gn.* 1:4, 10, 12, 18, 21, 25, 30.
128. *Gn.* 1:8.
129. *Gn.* 1:22.
130. Pl. *Ti.* 37C. See Ambr. *Hex.* 2.5.19–21; Aug. *Civ.* 11.21.
131. For example, *Ps.* 73:1: Ὡς ἀγαθὸς τῷ Ἰσραὴλ ὁ θεός.

Timaeus: "If so be that this Cosmos is beautiful [καλός] and its Constructor good [ἀγαθός], it is plain that he fixed his gaze on the Eternal [πρὸς τὸ ἀΐδιον]."[132] And it was only a further extension to apply to it as well the other formula of *Timaeus,* which followed almost immediately, that "the supreme originating principle of Becoming and the Cosmos" [γενέσεως καὶ κόσμου . . . ἀρχὴν κυριωτάτην] was that the Creator was good and was "devoid of envy."[133]

When this philosophical cosmogony of Athens encountered the nonphilosophical cosmogony of Jerusalem, many of the concepts of *Timaeus* put questions to the text of *Genesis* that had not been raised in quite that way before. In anticipation of that encounter, we have been reviewing the cosmogonic account in the *Timaeus* here with an eye on *Genesis.* As we continue the inquiry into Tertullian's question "What has Athens to do with Jerusalem?" and turn therefore to the cosmogonic account in *Genesis,* it will once again be a review of the one text in the light of the other.

---

132. Pl. *Ti.* 29A.
133. Pl. *Ti.* 29D–E.

III

Jerusalem: *Genesis* as a "Likely Account" (*Timaeus* 29D) of One God Almighty Maker

Regardless of what their doctrinal concepts about creation and the Creator may have been, ancient cosmogonies—including *De rerum natura*, *Timaeus*, and *Genesis*—presented themselves as accounts περὶ τοῦ παντὸς μέχρι γενέσεως ἀνθρωπίνης, as *Timaeus* called it,[1] explanations of the origins of the existing universe in the realm of becoming, up to and including the genesis of the human race. Thus it would seem that at one level of description the empirical components of the creation, as comprehended by *Genesis* in the phrase ὁ οὐρανὸς καὶ ἡ γῆ καὶ πᾶς ὁ κόσμος αὐτῶν,[2] as well as by *De rerum natura* in the similar phrase "of heaven and earth" [caeli . . . terraeque],[3] would have to be largely the same in all of them. Despite such obvious similarities between them, some of them quite illuminating and others really rather trivial, the components of the creation prove in other respects to have been quite different from one cosmogony to another. Therefore the counterpoint between *Genesis* and *Timaeus* made itself audible in both directions, not only through the general presuppositions of the two narratives but also, no less, through the specific details of their creation accounts, which would provide much of the subject matter for later interpretations. For the consideration of the concepts of creation in chapter 2 it was appropriate to allow the philosophical participant in the counterpoint, the *Timaeus* of Plato, to define the terms of the counterpoint. Conversely, for this examination of the components of creation it would seem to be sound, in the interest not only of reciprocity but of precision, to let the religious participant, the *Genesis* of Moses, set the outline and sequence, with each component being considered as it appeared for the first time in that account.

---

1. Pl. *Ti.* 90E.
2. *Gn.* 2:1.
3. Lucr. 5.245.

It is instructive in this connection to observe how often the presentation of *Timaeus* in English has made it virtually unavoidable to introduce some element from *Genesis* or another book of the Bible. Benjamin Jowett translated the final words of the dialogue (which will figure prominently in chapter 5 of this book), εἷς οὐρανὸς ὅδε μονογενὴς ὤν, as "the one only-begotten heaven," employing the translation of μονογενής in the Authorized Version of the Bible.[4] Francis M. Cornford criticized A.E. Taylor for making *Timaeus* "more modern (and considerably more Christian) than Herbert Spencer," but he felt obliged to explain *Timaeus* by observing that "myriads of Jews and Christians, from Moses to the present day, have believed that *in the beginning* God created the heavens and the earth, and have understood 'beginning' in a temporal sense."[5] Edith Hamilton, in her introduction to the reprinting of Jowett's translation of *Timaeus,* had to explain: "In the first chapter of Genesis, 'God said, Let there be light, and there was light.' That is not Plato's way of dealing with the matter. He thinks out what light is and how it must have come about. The chapter in Genesis is poetry; the *Timaeus* has a great deal of poetry in it, but its aim is science."[6] And R.G. Bury, in the introduction to his translation in the Loeb Classical Library (though not, it must be added, in the translation itself), paraphrased Plato's doctrine of primeval disorder as follows: "We are transported in imagination to a point 'before the beginning of years,' when time was not, and 'the earth was without form and void'"; thus he combined a passage from *Timaeus* with a passage from the Authorized Version of *Genesis.*[7] Also, where *Timaeus,* speaking about the origin of woman, referred to what happened "in the second becoming" [ἐν τῇ δευτέρᾳ γενέσει], Bury offered the translation "at their second incarnation."[8]

Attention to *Genesis* for a consideration of the components of creation commends itself as well because, although there were commentaries also on *Timaeus*—most notably for our purposes here that of Calcidius in the fourth century (addressed in chapter 6), but also those of the Neoplatonists Proclus and Jamblichos, and centuries later that of the Byzantine philosopher Michael Psellus—most of the subsequent interpretations of the similarities and differences between the two cosmogonies have taken

4. Pl. *Ti.* 92C; Jowett 1953, 3:780; *Jn.* 1:14, 1:18, 3:16, 3:18 (AV).
5. Cornford 1957, x, 27 n.
6. Hamilton and Cairns 1961, 1151.
7. Bury 1929, 5; Pl. *Ti.* 37E; *Gn.* 1:2 (AV).
8. Pl. *Ti.* 90E; Bury 1929, 249.

the literary form of commentaries on *Genesis*, beginning with the *De opificio* and the *Legum allegoria* of Philo, and extending to the treatises entitled *Hexaemeron* by Basil, Gregory of Nyssa, and Ambrose and to the three successive works by Augustine bearing the title *De Genesi*. Among portions of *Timaeus* that found no explicit counterpart in *Genesis* at all were the disquisitions on the physiology and anatomy of the liver, spleen, and other organs and on weight and movement.[9] Its discussion of the primacy of "sight" [ὄψις] in comparison with the other senses had an importance far beyond the anatomical and physiological; for to it was attributed "research into the nature of the Universe," together with "Philosophy in all its range, than which no greater boon has ever come or will come, by divine bestowal [δωρηθὲν ἐκ θεῶν], unto the race of mortals."[10] But there was no corresponding consideration of the senses in *Genesis*. That discussion, moreover, could have stimulated its Christian interpreters to a consideration of the relative importance of sight and hearing in both the Old Testament and the New Testament, where the patriarchs, prophets, and apostles did have visions, but where the word of God, perceived by "hearing" [ἀκοή] and responded to by "obedience" [ὑπακοή], claimed the primacy reserved for "sight" [ὄψις] in *Timaeus*; for as the New Testament said, summarizing the emphasis of the Old Testament as well, "faith cometh by hearing [ἡ πίστις ἐξ ἀκοῆς], and hearing by the word of God."[11]

Basic Questions of Cosmogony

As most subsequent interpreters were to learn, often to their dismay, the stark simplicity of the opening words of *Genesis*, "In the beginning God made the heaven and the earth" [!Εν ἀρχῇ ἐποίησεν ὁ θεὸς τὸν οὐρανὸν καὶ τὴν γῆν],[12] was really not so simple at all, for it left unaddressed some of the most basic questions of cosmogony. This was, as Gerhard Von Rad has put it, "not an independent theological chapter, but part of a great . . . dogmatic outline."[13] In its literary form, that sentence could be taken as a

---

9. Pl. *Ti.* 70D–71D, 62C–63E; on weight, see O'Brien 1984, 153–65.

10. Pl. *Ti.* 47A–E. On the interpretation of the senses in *Timaeus,* see also Vlastos 1981, 366–73.

11. *Rom.* 10:17 (AV).

12. *Gn.* 1:1.

13. Von Rad 1958, 143; see also Anderson 1955.

description of the first in a series of discrete creative actions, according to which the creation of the entire universe of "heaven and earth" took place on the first day, to be followed by the acts of creating the several beings, both living and nonliving, that were assigned to the several days of the hexaemeron. Or it could be seen as a comprehensive prefatory formula, a kind of chapter title under which the individual actions of each of the six days of creation were thereafter subsumed. Even more problematic for the history of cosmogonic speculation was the evident indifference of this sentence to the issue that Lucretius correctly identified as "the first principle," namely, "that no thing is ever by divine power produced from nothing" [nullam rem e nilo gigni diuinitus umquam]—the problem of "creatio ex nihilo."[14] The Greek version even appears to have made that issue more problematic still by its choice of verb. The Hebrew text employed the verb בָּרָא, which in the Hebrew Bible denoted the exclusive prerogative of God the Creator, and which, beginning with the "factors tending to the doctrine of *creatio ex nihilo* in Judaism"[15] and continuing with the subsequent development of this doctrine (especially in Christian theology), acquired the additional connotation of "creatio ex nihilo," though it does not seem to have originally possessed it in *Genesis*. But the verb in the Septuagint is not ἔκτισεν (although the verb κτίζειν came to carry a similar connotation in Greek) but ἐποίησεν; the Greek version contents itself with a general term, ποιεῖν, which corresponded to the general Hebrew verb עָשָׂה, a term applicable to many kinds of making, whether divine or human.[16]

Even if the verb meaning "to create," whether ποιεῖν or κτίζειν, did not necessarily imply the doctrine of "creatio ex nihilo," it in any case raised the issue of "materia ex qua" and, more specifically, in the question of Lucretius, "quattuor ex rebus si cuncta creantur."[17] As noted earlier, the idea of the four elements as the basic stuff of which all other things were made had come from Empedocles and possibly from other pre-Socratics as well. But apparently it owed its codification in the form of the doctrine of στοιχεῖα to the *Theaetetus* of Plato; and it owed much of its dissemination to its inclusion in Plato's *Timaeus* as a technical term, "elements of the Universe" [στοιχεῖα τοῦ παντός] (albeit with the later caveat that the term was quite inappropriate for "the man who has even a grain of sense"

---

14. Lucr. 1.149–50.
15. May 1994, 21–22.
16. Bauer 455–56, 680–81; Lampe 782–83, 1107.
17. Lucr. 1.763.

[ὑπὸ τοῦ καὶ βραχὺ φρονοῦντος]),[18] because of the circulation achieved by this dialogue in both East and West:

> Now that which has come into existence must needs be of bodily form [σωματοειδές], visible and tangible; yet without fire nothing could ever become visible, nor tangible without some solidity, nor solid without earth. Hence, in beginning to construct the body of the All, God was making it of fire and earth [ὅθεν ἐκ πυρὸς καὶ γῆς τὸ τοῦ παντὸς ἀρχόμενος ξυνιστάναι σῶμα ὁ θεὸς ἐποίει]. . . . Thus it was that in the midst between fire and earth God set water and air [οὕτω δὴ πυρός τε καὶ γῆς ὕδωρ ἀέρα τε ὁ θεὸς ἐν μέσῳ θείς], and having bestowed upon them so far as possible a like ratio one towards another—air being to water as fire to air, and water being to earth as air to water—he joined together and constructed a Heaven visible and tangible [οὐρανὸν ὁρατὸν καὶ ἁπτόν].[19]

Later on, however, *Timaeus* went on to specify "that fire and earth and water and air are solid bodies."[20] But otherwise the elements "are placed ceremoniously on their metaphysical pedestals, only to be left there, and quietly ignored in the rest of the treatise where the workings of nature are explored."[21] So nearly unavoidable has the concept of "elements" become that even where the word στοιχεῖα is absent from Plato's Greek text, it appears in English translation: "Now of the four *elements* the construction of the Cosmos had taken up the whole of every one" is Bury's rendering of the Greek Τῶν δὲ δὴ τεττάρων ἓν ὅλον ἕκαστον εἴληφεν ἡ τοῦ κόσμου ξύστασις.[22] The explanation in *Genesis* of ὁ οὐρανὸς καὶ ἡ γῆ, which were constructed by God to be no less "visible and tangible" than Plato's, did not rest on an analogous catalog of preexistent building blocks. Nevertheless, all four of the Empedoclean-Platonic ῥιζώματα-στοιχεῖα did somehow put in an appearance within its first three verses: !Ἐν ἀρχῇ ἐποίησεν ὁ θεὸς τὸν οὐρανὸν [air] καὶ τὴν γῆν [earth]. ἡ δὲ γῆ ἦν ἀόρατος καὶ ἀκατασκεύαστος, καὶ σκότος ἐπάνω τῆς ἀβύσσου, καὶ πνεῦμα θεοῦ [air again] ἐπεφέρετο ἐπάνω τοῦ ὕδατος [water]. καὶ εἶπεν ὁ θεὸς Γενηθήτω φῶς [fire]. καὶ ἐγένετο φῶς.[23] With such an identification of πνεῦμα as a

---

18. Pl. *Ti.* 48B.
19. Pl. *Ti.* 31B, 32B. See Schulz 1966, 25–31.
20. Pl. *Ti.* 53C.
21. Vlastos 1981, 108–9; see also Hirsch 1971, 372–75.
22. Pl. *Ti.* 32C; Bury 1929, 60–61.
23. *Gn.* 1:1–3.

biblical equivalent for "air" in the Timaean scheme, that parallel would go on to be used by Augustine as a justification for the use of the doctrine of the four elements as an interpretive tool for making sense of *Genesis*, even when "creatio ex nihilo" had come to be assumed as the primary meaning of the verb *create*.[24] Similarly, the description of "the spherical form of the All" [τὸ τοῦ παντὸς σχῆμα . . . σφαιροειδές] in *Timaeus* could be considered compatible with the description in *Genesis* of the στερέωμα, "firmamentum" or "dome," that God used to divide the water of heaven from the water of earth, calling it οὐρανός;[25] according to *Timaeus*, the term πᾶς οὐρανός could be used synonymously with κόσμος.[26]

Primeval Chaos

Any reader coming to the cosmogony of *Genesis* from having read the cosmogony of *Timaeus*, as we have done here—reading them, therefore, not in the sequence in which they were written, but in the sequence in which they appeared in Greek, and then again in the sequence in which they appeared in Latin—would look for equivalents in *Genesis*, if any, to the fundamental distinction of *Timaeus* between "what is perceptible to the senses [τὸ αἰσθητόν]" and "what is apprehensible only to the mind [τὸ νοητόν]."[27] The question raised earlier, whether the first verse of the *Genesis* account was intended only to provide a chapter title or to describe the first in a chronological series of acts of creation, could be relevant to such a distinction; for if it was a chapter title, it could be interpreted as having intended to make that very distinction by the phrase ὁ οὐρανὸς καὶ ἡ γῆ, with οὐρανός (heaven) standing for κόσμος νοητός and γῆ (earth) for κόσμος αἰσθητός; this was how Philo took it.[28] The interpretation of the opening words was crucial as well for the interpretation of what followed, ἡ δὲ γῆ ἦν ἀόρατος καὶ ἀκατασκεύαστος, καὶ σκότος ἐπάνω τῆς ἀβύσσου,[29] just as it was for the interpretation of the corresponding passage early in *Timaeus*, "When he took over all that was visible, seeing that it was not in a state of rest but in a state of discordant and disorderly motion, he brought it into order out of disorder [εἰς τάξιν . . . ἐκ τῆς ἀταξίας]."[30] A

---

24. Aug. *Civ.* 8.11.
25. Pl. *Ti.* 44D; *Gn.* 1:6–8.
26. Pl. *Ti.* 28B.
27. Pl. *Ti.* 28A.
28. Phil. *Leg. all.* 1.1.
29. *Gn.* 1:22.
30. Pl. *Ti.* 30A.

later passage of *Timaeus* described this "disorder" in detail, with "every variety of appearance" and movement "in various directions."[31] Both cosmogonies were confronted here by a primeval form of the perennial dilemma of theodicy; for "if so be that this Cosmos is beautiful and its Constructor good" [εἰ μὲν δὴ καλός ἐστιν ὅδε ὁ κόσμος ὅ τε δημιουργὸς ἀγαθός],[32] as *Timaeus* put it but as *Genesis* could also have put it, if in fact, as the dialogue immediately went on to specify, both of those adjectives more appropriately belonged in the superlative, so that the Creator was "most good" [ἄριστος] and this cosmos "most beautiful" [κάλλιστος],[33] then where in the world, where in such a world, could such chaos ever have come from?[34] If it came from the Creator, his goodness could be questioned; if it did not, his status as creator could be questioned. *Timaeus* had an easier time dealing with the dilemma, because its entire middle section, "What Comes of Necessity,"[35] provided it with a set of categories, particularly the two kinds of causes, "the necessary and the divine" [τὸ μὲν ἀναγκαῖον, τὸ δὲ θεῖον], for coping even with chaos.[36] By contrast, when a later prophet of Israel declared that God "shaped the earth and made it" but "did not create it to be chaos,"[37] he was making clear that such a resolution of the dilemma was not readily available to those who stood in the tradition of *Genesis*, which would not allow drawing a distinction of this kind between "necessary" causes and "divine" causes, because its picture of the process of creation was predicated on the monergism of the divine agency of the one God confessed in the Shema.[38]

In *Timaeus* the divine response to this chaos was to "bring it into order out of disorder" [εἰς τάξιν . . . ἐκ τῆς ἀταξίας],[39] but in the Septuagint *Genesis* the chaos was described as "invisible and unfinished" [ἀόρατος καὶ ἀκατασκεύαστος], with its most specific characteristic identified as "darkness over the abyss" [σκότος ἐπάνω τῆς ἀβύσσου]. Therefore, "God said, 'Let there be light'; and there was light."[40] Once again, *Genesis* left unanswered the question of whence and how the darkness had come into

---

31. Pl. *Ti.* 52D–53C.
32. Pl. *Ti.* 29A.
33. Pl. *Ti.* 30A.
34. See Scheffel 1976, 71–74.
35. Pl. *Ti.* 47E–61A; on Necessity, see Brisson 1974, 469–78.
36. Pl. *Ti.* 68E.
37. *Is.* 45:18 (NJB).
38. Gunkel 1895 remains, a full century later, an important examination of the similarities and differences between biblical and nonbiblical views of "chaos."
39. Pl. *Ti.* 30A.
40. *Gn.* 1:2–3.

being, concentrating instead on the miracle of light. The scientific discussion of light and darkness in *Timaeus* accounted for them on the basis of two of the four elements, fire and air—light from the first, darkness from the second. For in addition to the most familiar and common kind of fire, which was called "flame" [φλόξ], there was "the kind issuing from flame, which does not burn but supplies light to the eyes" [φῶς δὲ τοῖς ὄμμασι παρέχει].[41] Thus the eyes were "light-bearing" [θωσφόρα ὄμματα], through which "the pure fire within us" was emitted "in a smooth and dense stream," making vision possible by the action of "like unto like" [ὅμοιον πρὸς ὅμοιον].[42] Air, too, was of various kinds, among which there was "the most translucent kind which is called by the name of aether" [τὸ μὲν εὐαγέστατον ἐπίκλην αἰθὴρ καλούμενος] and which did not obstruct the flow of light from the light-bearing eyes.[43] The particles thrown off from an object that were of the same size as the particles of the "visual stream" [τὸ τῆς ὄψεως ῥεῦμα] itself were therefore "imperceptible" [ἀναίσθητα] and were called "transparent" [διαφανῆ], whereas the particles that were either larger or smaller were black or white or some color in between.[44] The opposite kind of air was "the most opaque" and was called "mist and darkness" [ὁ δὲ θολερώτατος ὁμίχλη τε καὶ σκότος].[45] In this way the concept of the four στοιχεῖα enabled Plato to cope in *Timaeus* with the relation between "light" and "darkness" by treating them under distinct categories; in contrast, the creation account of *Genesis* made them the subject of the primeval cosmic drama of "Fiat lux!"

The apostle Paul affirmed a direct continuity between his gospel and that cosmic drama, while also espousing a version of the relation between the inner and the outer light, when he declared: "The same God who said, 'Out of darkness let light shine,' has caused his light to shine within us, to give the light of revelation—the revelation of the glory of God in the face of Jesus Christ."[46] Opposing the notion of such a continuity between creation and redemption by "the same God," later Christian dualisms were able to find in these verses of *Genesis* a biblical justification for their fundamental intuition that from the very beginning there had been a conflict between the power of darkness and the power of light, with the world of creatures, especially of human creatures, caught more or less

41. Pl. *Ti.* 58C.
42. Pl. *Ti.* 45B–C; Aug. *Trin.* 9.3.3.
43. Pl. *Ti.* 58D.
44. Pl. *Ti.* 67D–E.
45. Pl. *Ti.* 58D.
46. 2 *Cor.* 4:6.

helplessly between the two contending forces. In response, Christian orthodoxy quoted these words of Paul to affirm the continuity.[47] Eventually,
and with considerable help from the Platonic tradition, it went on to
develop the argument that as darkness was the absence of light rather than
a positive reality in its own right, so, more generally evil was to be defined
as a "privatio boni" rather than as a second god;[48] this definition became
orthodox despite Paul's use, in the passage just quoted, of the portentous
term "the god of this passing age" [ὁ θεὸς τοῦ αἰῶνος τούτου][49] as a title
for the devil. In *Genesis* the presence of evil was not tied directly to
darkness as opposed to light but attributed, in the story of the temptation,
to the person of the "crafty" serpent.[50] Eventually the two explanations
of evil came together, with the identification of the serpent as the devil and
the reliance of the *Gospel of John* on the metaphor of light and darkness
as one of its most important theological themes for the conflict between
good and evil.

A more direct function of darkness and light in the *Genesis* narrative
itself, and one that also invited a much more contrapuntal treatment of
Timaeus, was the measurement of time, "night and day."[51] Though not a
momentous analogy, it does deserve mention that in the language both of
Genesis and of *Timaeus* there appeared the sequence of first "evening" or
"night" and then "morning" or "day," rather than the other way
around.[52] A curious feature of the first chapter of *Genesis,* which has
proved especially puzzling to those interpreters who have striven to read it
as a literal account of events that took place at a definite time in history
and in the course of six days of normal length—and which those opposed
to such a literal interpretation could cite as proof against it—was that
God's separating "light from darkness" and calling "the light day, and the
darkness night" was followed immediately by the formula "So evening
came, and morning came, the first day [or, in the Septuagint, one day,
ἡμέρα μία]."[53] For not until the fourth day would God make the sun and
moon "to separate day from night," which raised the troubling question
of what the word *day* could be supposed to mean until then. With the

47. Tert. *Marc.* 5.11.
48. Aug. *Gen. imp.* 5.
49. 2 *Cor.* 4:4.
50. *Gn.* 3:1.
51. See Callahan 1948 and the discussions of time in *Timaeus* in Matter 1964, 132–36,
and Gloy 1986, 48–74.
52. *Gn.* 1:5; Pl. *Ti.* 39C.
53. *Gn.* 1:4–5.

events of this fourth day of creation, whatever the system of measuring days had been before that, there finally were, according to *Genesis*, "two great lights, the greater to govern the day and the lesser to govern the night"; though they were not given names in *Genesis*, as they were in many ancient cosmogonies (including both *De rerum natura* and *Timaeus*), they were to "serve as signs both for festivals and for seasons and years."[54] *Timaeus*, too, specified such indications for its measurements of time: "Night and Day, which are the revolution of the one and most intelligent circuit [of the sun]; and Month, each time that the Moon having completed her own orbit overtakes the Sun; and Year, as often as the Sun has completed his own orbit."[55] To this natural calendar of day, month, and year *Genesis* added its own special component, the sacred week, which became the distinctive way of marking the six days of divine creation and the seventh day of divine rest on the Sabbath.[56] Although the Sabbath was based here on the creation, which was shared by the entire human race and the entire universe, so that Philo could identify it as "the birthday of the cosmos" [τοῦ κόσμου γενέθλιος],[57] it was in fact a part of the Jewish liturgical calendar. Another parallel to *Timaeus* was the use in *Genesis* of the lapidary phrase "With them he made the stars" to explain the origin of the vast range of heavenly bodies, which were for both *Timaeus* and *Genesis* too numerous to count,[58] and which were incidental to both cosmogonies.

Imago Dei

One of the most striking contrasts between *Genesis* and *Timaeus*, and also between the "E" account in the first chapter of *Genesis* and the "J" account in the second chapter, made its presence felt in the creation of man. For (in the words of *Timaeus*) "as regards the mode in which the rest of living creatures have been produced,"[59] chapter 1 of *Genesis* made the human race the apex of creation by telling the story of the creation of the other living beings first, with man as the climax on the sixth and final day; *Timaeus* did so by following its account of the creation of man with a

---

54. *Gn.* 1:14–19.
55. Pl. *Ti.* 39C; Claghorn 1954, 84–98; Mohr 1985, 55–75.
56. *Gn.* 2:2–3; *Ex.* 20:8–11.
57. Phil. *Opif.* 89.
58. *Gn.* 15:5.
59. Pl. *Ti.* 90E.

description of the several genera of animals (as well as woman) as various forms of punishment for men who had gone wrong; and chapter 2 of *Genesis* began with the creation of man: "In the day in which the Lord God made the heaven and the earth, and every herb of the field before it was on the earth . . . God formed the man of the dust of the earth."[60] For the purposes of this study of the counterpoint in subsequent history, that contrast had several direct implications.

First of these in order of mention within the unified account, and foremost in importance for the history of the counterpoint, was the doctrine of the "imago Dei," the creation of man by God "in our image, after our likeness" [κατ᾽ εἰκόνα ἡμετέραν καὶ καθ᾽ ὁμοίωσιν],[61] which, according to one twentieth-century theological critic, "formed a synthesis between the Platonic-Aristotelian-Stoic view and the Christian view of man, which dominated the whole of the Patristic period and the Christian Middle Ages, and has been, and still is, operative."[62] For all the momentous significance it would be asked to carry throughout the history of its interpretation, the concept of "imago Dei" was, curiously, left without specific content here at its first appearance. *Genesis* referred to it in its genealogy—"On the day when God created man he made him in the likeness of God"—then went on in the next verse to explain that Adam "begot a son in his likeness and image, and named him Seth"; once again, there was no particular content indicated.[63] The next reference in *Genesis* to the "imago Dei" invoked it as a reinforcement of the prohibition of murder: "He that sheds the blood of a man, for that man his blood shall be shed; for in the image of God has God made man."[64] This moral application of the concept was to persist in the New Testament,[65] which, however, also made it into a technical term of Christology when it identified Christ as the one "who is the very image of God" [ὅς ἐστιν εἰκὼν τοῦ θεοῦ],[66] affecting the reading both of *Genesis* and of *Timaeus* by Christian theologians. The identification of Christ as the image of God in person legitimized the process of going beyond the simply moral application to a doctrine of the divine image that could fill it with the meaning provided by the humanity of Jesus Christ as the perfect man.

60. *Gn.* 2:4–7.
61. *Gn.* 1:26.
62. Brunner 1939, 92–93.
63. *Gn.* 5:2–3.
64. *Gn.* 9:6.
65. *Jas.* 3:9.
66. 2 *Cor.* 4:4.

But a complementary method for finding such meaning, alongside both the moral and the Christological, came from the full-blown counterpart to the biblical notion of "imago Dei" that was provided by the Platonic writings, most dramatically by *Timaeus*. Its closing words, "image of the [God who is] apprehensible only to the mind; God made perceptible to the senses; most great and most good, most beautiful and most perfect in His generation—even this one only-begotten Heaven" [εἰκὼν τοῦ νοητοῦ θεὸς αἰσθητός, μέγιστος καὶ ἄριστος κάλλιστός τε καὶ τελεώτατος γέγονεν εἷς οὐρανὸς ὅδε μονογενὴς ὤν],[67] all of which later became technical terms in Christian theology, were a summary and a climax of its central theme of creation according to the image of the Eternal. As noted earlier, that theme made use of the same term that appeared in the Septuagint of *Genesis*, "image" [εἰκών], whose correlative in *Timaeus*, though not in *Genesis*, was "model" [παράδειγμα];[68] the other term in *Genesis*, ὁμοίωσις, was likewise present in *Timaeus*, in the general thesis, attributed to "the God," the Demiurge, "that the similar is infinitely more beautiful than the dissimilar" [μυρίῳ κάλλιον ὅμοιον ἀνομοίου], which was the basis of the Demiurge's decision to make the world spherical, "which of all shapes is the most perfect and the most self-similar."[69] For *Genesis* the model of the image was God the Creator, for *Timaeus* "that which is uniform"; but for both cosmogonies the concept of the image was a way of saying that "that object must of necessity be beautiful [καλόν]."[70] The subject of the predicate *image of God* in *Genesis* was specifically humanity rather than the universe as a whole, but in subsequent exegesis and speculation it was not difficult to broaden that predicate to make it coextensive with the predicate καλός, which was applied, in *Genesis* no less than in *Timaeus*, both to humanity and to the universe as a whole. Therefore the message of both cosmogonies was that "If so be that this Cosmos is beautiful [καλός] and its Constructor [δημιουργός] good [ἀγαθός], it is plain that he fixed his gaze on the Eternal [πρὸς τὸ αἴδιον],"[71] creating it according to his image. Nevertheless it was true of both comogonies that the doctrine of creation, and therefore the doctrine of creation "according to the image" [κατ᾽ εἰκόνα], pertained in a special sense to the creation of humanity.

The uniqueness of the creation of humanity was emphasized in the

---

67. Pl. *Ti.* 92C (adapted from Jowett).
68. Pl. *Ti.* 29B.
69. Pl. *Ti.* 33B.
70. Pl. *Ti.* 28A.
71. Pl. *Ti.* 29A.

second version of the creation story of *Genesis* by the words "God formed the man of dust of the earth, and breathed upon his face the breath of life, and the man became a living soul" [καὶ ἐγένετο ὁ ἄνθρωπος εἰς ψυχὴν ζῶσαν].[72] Earlier it had spoken of "every reptile creeping on the earth, which has in itself a soul of life" [ὃ ἔχει ἐν ἑαυτῷ ψυχὴν ζωῆς],[73] which makes it clear that the Greek term ψυχή, like its Hebrew original נֶפֶשׁ, pertained not only to "the man" but to other living creatures. Nevertheless, there was apparently a difference between the man and other creatures, in that other creatures were said to "have" [ἔχειν] a ψυχή, whereas the man was said to "have become" [ἐγένετο] one. Only concerning the creation of the man, moreover, did *Genesis* in its first account speak of an express divine decision and a consultation of God (something like what *Timaeus* called a λογισμός)[74] with himself, or perhaps with the angels— "Let us make man"[75]—rather than of a simple and direct divine fiat. And then, in its second account, *Genesis* posited a process for the creation of the man consisting of two distinct stages (prior to the separate creation of the woman, which was to follow later): first, "God formed the man" [ἔπλασεν ὁ θεὸς τὸν ἄνθρωπον], a process that seemed to pertain only to the human body, although the text did not say that in so many words; second, "[God] breathed upon his face the breath of life" [ἐνεφύσησεν εἰς τὸ πρόσωπον αὐτοῦ πνοὴν ζωῆς]. Only after the second stage, according to the text, did "the man became a living soul." The two accounts would provide Philo with textual justification for his fundamental distinction between two creations of humanity. *Genesis* did not, here or elsewhere, present any schematization of the relation between body and soul or between either of these and spirit; and even in the New Testament the entire schematism was sufficiently vague—for example, in the relation between ἡ ψυχή μου and τὸ πνεῦμά μου in the Magnificat[76]—to provoke later debates over dichotomy versus trichotomy. Yet there is no warrant in the text of *Genesis* to conclude that the sequence of the two stages implied a priority of worth for the body over the soul, rather than the other way around.

Although a priority of worth for the soul over the body may have been no more than hinted at in the account of the creation of man in *Genesis*, it

72. *Gn.* 2:7.
73. *Gn.* 2:30.
74. Pl. *Ti.* 34A–B.
75. *Gn.* 1:26.
76. *Lk.* 1:46–47.

became unambiguous in the account of the creation of the world soul in *Timaeus*.[77] In recounting "the reasoning of the ever-existing God concerning the god which was one day to be existent" [ἀεὶ λογισμὸς θεοῦ περὶ τὸν ποτὲ ἐσόμενον θεόν], it spoke first about "a whole and perfect body compounded of perfect bodies." Only then did it go on to describe how "in the midst thereof He set Soul, which He stretched throughout the whole of it, and therewith He enveloped also the exterior of its body."[78] Here, too, just as in chapter 2 of *Genesis*, there would seem to be a σῶμα, a body that first was formed and only then infused with whatever was necessary for a ψυχή to animate it. Unlike *Genesis*, however, *Timaeus* immediately went on to supply what Archer-Hind calls the "rectification of an inexact statement" by explaining that "as regards the Soul, although we are essaying to describe it after the body, God did not likewise plan it to be younger than the body"; on the contrary, "God constructed Soul to be older than Body and prior in birth and excellence [γενέσει καὶ ἀρετῇ προτέραν καὶ πρεσβυτέραν], since she was to be the mistress and ruler."[79] As A.E. Taylor has fittingly paraphrased this passage:

> It must not be inferred from our having first spoken of the formation of the body of the οὐρανός and then of the soul which God "put into it" that this represents the real order of creation. In speaking as we did, we fell into a neglect of accuracy and order which is one of our human infirmities. The world did not begin by being a body and then become a *living* body. We ought to have put the soul first, because soul comes before body γενέσει καὶ ἀρετῇ "in order both of becoming and of worth."[80]

In corroboration of this emphasis, Plato affirmed at least twice in book 10 of the *Laws:* "Truly and finally, then, it would be a most veracious and complete statement to say that we find soul has to be prior to body, and body secondary and posterior, soul governing and body being governed according to the ordinance of nature."[81] At the hands of later biblical interpreters, both Jewish and Christian, the account of the sequence of body and soul in *Genesis* would easily lend itself to the more detailed

---

77. See Scheffel 1976, 91–117.
78. Pl. *Ti.* 34A–B.
79. Archer-Hind 1888, 104 n. 9; Pl. *Ti.* 34B–C.
80. Taylor 1928, 105.
81. Pl. *Leg.* 10.896B–C, 892A–B.

explanation in *Timaeus,* on the basis of this Platonic theory of body and soul as expounded in the *Laws* and elsewhere.

Moral Choice

There was something of a parallel between *Genesis* and *Timaeus* on another score as well. For the account of the formation of the man out of the dust of the earth and of his having become a living soul was followed immediately in *Genesis* by the assignment of moral choice: "And the Lord God gave a charge [ἐνετείλατο] to Adam, saying, 'Of every tree which is in the garden *thou* mayest eat for food [βρώσει φαγῇ], but of the tree of learning the knowledge of beautiful and evil [γινώσκειν καλὸν καὶ πονηρόν]—of it *ye* shall not eat [οὐ φάγεσθε].'"[82] It is a linguistic curiosity, though perhaps no more than that, that in the Greek translation, but not in the Hebrew original, the positive permission was put in the singular whereas the negative prohibition was put in the plural. Another translation, and one of perhaps greater importance for the subsequent history of the counterpoint between *Genesis* and *Timaeus,* was the designation of the forbidden fruit as coming from "the tree of learning the knowledge of good and evil" [τὸ ξύλον τοῦ εἰδέναι γνωστὸν καλοῦ καὶ πονηροῦ].[83] For this emphasis on γνωστόν in the determination of moral choice, unaccompanied as it was by more detailed explanation, helped to make possible a connection with that most Socratic of moral concepts, the equation of moral wrong with ignorance, familiar from many of the Platonic dialogues. In *Timaeus* this equation took the form of identifying ignorance as "the worst of maladies"[84] and of asserting, "And indeed almost all those affections which are called by way of reproach 'incontinence in pleasure,' as though the wicked acted voluntarily, are wrongly so reproached; for no one is voluntarily wicked [κακὸς μὲν γὰρ ἑκὼν οὐδείς], but the wicked man becomes wicked by reason of some evil condition of body and unskilled nurture [διὰ ἀπαίδευτον τροφήν], and these are experiences which are hateful to everyone and involuntary."[85]

As in *Genesis,* in *Timaeus* the account of the formation of the souls "equal in number to the stars" by the Demiurge is followed with a moral revelation: "He showed them the nature of the Universe, and declared unto them the laws of destiny [τὴν τοῦ παντὸς φύσιν ἔδειξε, νόμους τε

82. *Gn.* 2:16–17. On καλόν and ἀγαθόν as "synonyms," see Gloy 1986, 18 n. 14.
83. *Gn.* 2:9.
84. Pl. *Ti.* 44C.
85. Pl. *Ti.* 86D–E.

τοὺς εἱμαρμένους εἶπεν αὐταῖς],—namely, how that the first birth should be one and the same ordained for all, in order that none might be slighted by Him." Each soul was then "sown into his own proper organ of time," a star, so that it might grow into "the most god-fearing of living creatures" [ζώων τὸ θεοσεβέστατον].[86] Even earlier, *Timaeus* had, moreover, also drawn a clear linkage between morality and cosmogony: "With regard to wisdom [περὶ τῆς φρονήσεως], you perceive, no doubt, the law here,— how much attention it has devoted from the very beginning to the Cosmic Order, by discovering all the effects which the divine causes produce upon human life."[87] Yet those were not the only considerations of moral choice in the *Timaeus,* which also addressed the problem of "fear and anger and all such emotions as are naturally allied thereto." With respect to these, there was a clear moral choice: "If they shall master these they will live justly, but if they are mastered [by them, they will live] unjustly" [ὧν εἰ μὲν κρατήσοιεν, δίκῃ βιώσοιντο, κρατηθέντες δὲ ἀδικίᾳ].[88] For in this sense it was possible for "the mortal creature" [τὸ θνητόν], by allowing fear and anger to master it, to "become the cause of its own evils."[89] One of those evils was that whereas "he that has lived his appointed time well shall return again to his abode in his native star, and shall gain a life that is blessed and congenial [βίον εὐδαίμονα καὶ συνήθη]," there was punishment awaiting "whoso has failed therein: [he] shall be changed into woman's nature at the second birth."[90] This form of punishment was in keeping with the statement a little earlier "that, since human nature is two-fold, the superior sex is that which hereafter should be designated 'man' [ἀνήρ]."[91]

In the dramaturgy of the *Genesis* account, it may in a sense be said that when "the Lord God gave a charge [ἐνετείλατο] to Adam," that was a prelude to the story of the fall. By a strictly chronological reading, the creation of the woman came after the "charge" but before the transgression, so that the textually unwarranted but theologically justifiable grammatical shift in the Septuagint from the singular "thou mayest eat for food" [βρώσει φαγῇ] to the plural "ye shall not eat" [οὐ φάγεσθε][92] was not only proleptic but portentous, considering how it all turned out. And

---

86. Pl. *Ti.* 41E.
87. Pl. *Ti.* 24B–C.
88. Pl. *Ti.* 42B.
89. Pl. *Ti.* 42E.
90. Pl. *Ti.* 42B.
91. Pl. *Ti.* 42A.
92. *Gn.* 2:16–17.

even though, strictly speaking, the prohibition as it stood had, at least in
the text, been addressed not to her but only to the man, the woman's
paraphrase of it to the serpent was in the plural (in the Greek and also in
the original Hebrew this time): "God said, 'Ye shall not eat of it, neither
shall ye touch it' [οὐ φάγεσθε ἀπ᾽ αὐτοῦ, οὐδὲ μὴ ἅψησθε αὐτοῦ]."[93] (Eve
added the latter prohibition of even touching the tree to the earlier commandment as issued to Adam.) It would be attractive, in the light of later
history, to read the response of the tempter to Eve, "God knew [ᾔδει γὰρ ὁ
θεός] that in whatever day ye should eat of it your eyes would be opened,
and ye would be as gods, knowing good and evil [ἔσεσθε ὡς θεοί, γινώσ
κοντες καλὸν καὶ πονηρόν]," in relation to the dictum of *Timaeus* that "No
one is voluntarily wicked" [κακὸς μὲν γὰρ ἑκὼν οὐδείς];[94] but there appears to be no direct justification for such a bold interpretation. Considerably less audacious would be the reading of the words "the Lord God gave
a charge [ἐνετείλατο]" in *Genesis* in connection with the explanation of
Timaeus that "He had fully declared unto them all these ordinances, to the
end that He might be blameless in respect of the future wickedness of any
one of them [ἵνα τῆς ἔπειτα εἴη κακίας ἑκάστων ἀναίτιος]."[95] For this
explanation could be seen as a paraphrase of various biblical passages,
such as the prayer in the *Book of Psalms* "so that thou mayest be proved
right in thy charge and just in passing sentence."[96]

One of the most telling differences between the two accounts manifested itself in relation to this very issue of the connection between morality and creation, in the definition of the consequences of the wrong moral
choice and thus in the understanding of death. When the apostle Paul
wrote, "Sin pays a wage, and the wage is death,"[97] he was, as the context
of that statement within his larger comparison of Christ and Adam suggests, commenting on the threat with which the "charge" of the Lord God
to Adam (and Eve) concluded: "In whatever day ye eat of [the tree of
learning the knowledge of good and evil], ye shall die by death."[98] The
subsequent history of the concept of human mortality, notably the con-
troversy between Augustine and the Pelagians about whether it was a
natural condition or one that had been introduced into the human race by

---

93. *Gn.* 3:4.
94. Pl. *Ti.* 86D.
95. *Gn.* 2:16–17; Pl. *Ti.* 42D.
96. *Ps.* 51:4; see also *Rom.* 2:1–2.
97. *Rom.* 6:23.
98. *Gn.* 2:17.

the coming of sin,[99] made it clear that the specific meaning of the threat to Adam was by no means obvious: Adam and Eve did not "die by death" on the very day they ate of the forbidden fruit; Adam lived a total of 930 years, though it is not clear whether that term was intended to include the "time" between the creation and the fall, however long that may have been.[100] Many interpreters throughout the centuries have, therefore, taken the threatening words of the Lord God to Adam to mean, "In whatever day ye eat of [the tree of learning the knowledge of good and evil], ye shall become subject to death," that is, mortal rather than immortal as heretofore. It likewise bears pointing out that the account of the fall of Adam and Eve in chapter 3 of *Genesis* did not go on to play a significant explanatory role in the consideration of death or even of sin by Hebrew Scripture. Only in the New Testament—principally in the epistles of Paul (chapter 5 of *Romans* and chapter 15 of *1 Corinthians*)—was a causal connection posited between the disobedience in the Garden of Eden and the universality of death, which in most books of the Old Testament usually seemed to be treated as a "natural" phenomenon (although "natural" was not an indigenous category in those books).

For *Timaeus,* by contrast, the category of the natural was an important key to the understanding of the phenomenon of death. The term *nature* (φύσις) was employed early in the dialogue to refer to knowledge "about the nature of the Universe" [περὶ φύσεως τοῦ παντός].[101] Its central meaning as a norm of understanding and behavior has been summarized by A.E. Taylor: "φύσις = normal state or condition. For this common sense of the word cf. *infra*, 64 d 1 τὸ εἰς φύσιν ἀπιὸν πάλιν ἀθρόον ἡδύ, 'the return, on a sufficient scale, to one's normal condition is pleasant.'"[102] He goes on, in his comments on the closing passage of *Timaeus,* to describe it as "the main point of [Plato's] theory of φύσις, that 'passage' is the most fundamental character of 'Nature.'"[103] On the basis of those definitions of nature as a "normal state or condition" and as "passage," the interpretation of Plato's meaning here seems evident. It was based on a fundamental distinction between "every process which is contrary to nature" [πᾶν τὸ παρὰ φύσιν] and "that which takes place naturally" [τὸ δ' ᾗ πέφυκε γιγνόμενον]. There were, accordingly, two kinds of death. The first kind,

99. Aug. *Corrept.* 12.23.
100. *Gn.* 5:5.
101. Pl. *Ti.* 27A.
102. Taylor 1928, 421; he adds references to Arist. *Met.* .1015a13, and to Arist. *E.N.* K. 117eb.7.
103. Taylor 1928, 649.

"which occurs in consequence of disease or wounds, is painful" and contrary to nature. To explain it, the dialogue turned yet once more to the theory of the four elements, "earth, fire, water, and air," of which the body was composed. "Disorders and disease," consequently, could be said to result from "an excess or a deficiency of these elements" [τούτων ἡ παρὰ φύσιν πλεονεξία καὶ ἔνδεια]. By contrast, "that [death] which follows on old age and constitutes a natural end [τέλος κατὰ φύσιν] is the least grievous of deaths and is accompanied by more of pleasure than of pain."[104] A far closer parallel to the traditional interpretation of Genesis on this point was provided by the address of the Demiurge to the lesser gods. Identifying himself as their "framer and father" [δημιουργὸς πατήρ τε], he reminded them that they were "not wholly immortal or indissoluble." "Yet in no wise," he promised, "shall ye be dissolved nor incur the doom of death, seeing that in my will [τῆς ἐμῆς βουλήσεως] ye possess a bond greater and more sovereign than the bonds wherewith, at your birth, ye were bound together."[105] That emphasis of Timaeus on the decisiveness of the divine "will" for the issue of life or death in divine beings could be made to comport well with the statement of Genesis that "the Lord God gave a charge [ἐνετείλατο] to Adam" dealing with the same issue in human beings.

We have already considered the creation of woman in Genesis, because although the "charge" preceded the detailed account of it, she subsequently, to the serpent, described the charge as having been addressed also to her. Strictly speaking, moreover, the creation of woman had already been mentioned, though only in passing, as part of the work of the sixth day in the version of the creation story recounted by chapter 1: "And God made man, according to the image of God he made him [αὐτόν], male and female he made them [αὐτούς]."[106] But it does need to be mentioned here again, because the step-by-step narrative of her creation came only in chapter 2, after the step-by-step narrative of the forming of the man from "the dust of the earth." It was connected to the perceived need of the man for "a help appropriate to him" [βοηθὸν κατ' αὐτόν]. None of the animals was qualified to be "a help like to himself" [βοηθὸς ὅμοιος αὐτῷ]. Inducing in Adam the "ecstasy of a trance" [ἔκστασις], God fashioned a rib from Adam into a woman.[107] The location of this account, almost as an after-

---

104. Pl. Ti. 81E–82A.
105. Pl. Ti. 41A–B.
106. Gn. 1:27.
107. Gn. 2:18–3:1.

thought to the main body of the cosmogony of *Genesis,* was matched in the cosmogony of *Timaeus,* in what Cornford characterizes as an "appendix": "For as regards the mode in which the rest of living creatures have been produced we must make but a brief statement, seeing that there is no need to speak at length."[108] The first of these other "living creatures" was woman. The origin of "women and the whole female sex"[109] was accounted for in the context of what would take place "at their second becoming" [ἐν τῇ δευτέρᾳ γενέσει], which was a way of dealing with the deficiencies and delinquencies of the first birth: "According to the probable account, all those creatures generated as men who proved themselves cowardly and spent their lives in wrong-doing were transformed, at their second becoming, into women."[110] The subsequent development of Jewish and Christian thought about the relation between woman and man was significantly affected by these two "appendices" in *Genesis* and *Timaeus* and by the relation between them.

Both cosmogonies summarized their accounts somewhat before concluding them. In its present form, *Genesis* presented such a summary at the end of the first narrative ("E"), as a transition to the second ("J"): "And the heavens and the earth were finished, and the whole cosmos of them" [Καὶ συνετελέσθησαν ὁ οὐρανὸς καὶ ἡ γῆ καὶ πᾶς ὁ κόσμος αὐτῶν].[111] *Timaeus,* too, could say even before getting around to the creation of women, "And now the task prescribed for us at the beginning, to give a description of the Universe up to the production of mankind, would appear to be wellnigh completed."[112] These conclusions of the two cosmogonies also suggest, however, that the most fundamental component of creation, so fundamental that it could just as legitimately have been discussed as a "concept of creation" in our second chapter, was what Lucretius called the "caeli rationes ordine certo,"[113] the order of creation. Typically, *Timaeus* was a much richer source of vocabulary for this component than *Genesis,* even though in both accounts God "brought it into order out of disorder" [εἰς τάξιν . . . ἐκ τῆς ἀταξίας].[114] Both the vocabulary of this transitional conclusion in *Genesis,* above all of course, the momentous phraseology πᾶς ὁ κόσμος αὐτῶν, with the dual meaning of

108. Pl. *Ti.* 90E. Cornford 1957, 355.
109. Pl. *Ti.* 91D.
110. Pl. *Ti.* 90E (modified from Bury); see the comments of Archer-Hind 1888, 144 n. 4.
111. *Gn.* 2:1.
112. Pl. *Ti.* 90E.
113. Lucr. 1.1183–84.
114. Pl. *Ti.* 30A.

κόσμος as "universe" (as in the English word *cosmic*) and as "adornment" (as in the English word *cosmetics*), could be brought together in the concept of order, which justified the ongoing process of reading each of the two cosmogonies in the light of the other. The second half of this book addresses the history of that process, in the thought of the Hellenistic Judaism of Alexandria and then in the Christian theologies of New Rome and of Catholic Rome.

IV

Alexandria: The God of *Genesis* as "Maker and Father" (*Timaeus* 28C)

"What has Athens to do with Jerusalem?" The first to ask this question, with its negative or at best minimalist implications, was, as noted earlier, the Christian Tertullian in Roman North Africa at the end of the second century. But the first to answer the question, in considerably more maximalist fashion, had already been the Jews of Alexandria. They were also the first to study the counterpoint between the cosmogony of Athens in *Timaeus* and the cosmogony of Jerusalem in *Genesis,* which, except for any Jews of the Diaspora who may have continued to know Hebrew when they had acquired Greek,[1] it was not possible to study until *Genesis* was translated into Greek, because *Timaeus* had never been translated into Hebrew. So it was that the two cosmogonies first came together in Egypt, the very Egypt where, according to *Timaeus,* cosmogonic traditions had been preserved in "the most ancient" of "sacred writings";[2] where Moses, who wrote the cosmogony of *Genesis* and other "sacred writings" of Israel by divine inspiration, had been given "the nurture due a prince" as the supposed son of the Pharaoh's daughter, which would presumably have included the study of Egyptian science;[3] and where, by a widely circulated "Egyptian mirage," Plato himself was said by the church fathers to have studied.[4] The elective affinities were so predominant here that sometimes "it is . . . well-nigh impossible . . . to determine with precision which of the two traditions ultimately has the upper hand."[5] The documentation of these affinities comes from several sources, but above all from the writings of Philo of Alexandria, because "the large-scale use of the *Timaeus* for purposes of Biblical exegesis . . . is a personal

---

1. Nikiprowetzky 1977, 50–96, is a careful consideration pro and con of the question "Philon savait-il l'hébreu?"

2. Pl. *Ti.* 23E, 22E; see Bidez 1945, 21–23 and appendix 2, 19–40, on Atlantis.

3. Phil. *V. Mos.* 1.20; *Ac.* 7:22; Ambr. *Hex.* 1.2.6.

4. Clem. *Str.* 1.15.89; Tert. *Anim.* 2.10. Froidefond 1971 is a history of this "mirage."

5. Winston 1979, 21.

achievement of Philo";[6] the deuterocanonical *Book of Wisdom* in the Septuagint, which was also written in Alexandria and in Greek, and "almost 20% of [whose] total vocabulary [is] never found in any other canonical book of the Old Testament," including vocabulary that was almost certainly drawn from *Timaeus,* whether directly or indirectly;[7] and behind both of these, also originating in Alexandria "sometime in the third century B.C.E.," the Septuagint *Genesis* itself, which at the very least, as noted earlier, shared with its surrounding culture some of the vocabulary of *Timaeus*—whether or not the conventional scholarly wisdom, challenged by Elias Bickerman, is correct in attributing it to "Alexandrian Jews who no longer knew enough Hebrew to satisfy their religious needs."[8]

In his commentary on the creation story in *Genesis,* Philo freely quoted from Athens as well as from Jerusalem.[9] For example, the Sabbath, which *Genesis* had based on the universality of the creation rather than on the particularity of the covenant with Israel, was, Philo insisted, "the festival, not of a single city or country, but of the universe," and was the only festival worthy of the name "universal" because it was a celebration of nothing less than "the birthday of the cosmos" [τοῦ κόσμου γενέθλιος].[10] To prove this he invoked the authority of the Greek lawgiver Solon, who had divided human life into ten stages of seven years each, as well as the language of Rome, in which, by his etymology, the Latin *septem* was derived from the Greek σεβασμός (reverence).[11] That demonstrated to Philo "the honour in which [seven] is held by the most approved investigators of the science of Mathematics and Astronomy among Greeks and other peoples, and the special honour accorded to it by that lover of virtue Moses [ὑπὸ τοῦ φιλαρέτου Μωυσέως]" in his account of the creation.[12] And so Philo found it altogether natural to quote from Plato (including *Timaeus*) by name and also to quote *Timaeus* by referring to its author as "one of the men of old" [τῶν ἀρχαίων τις] without identifying him.[13]

---

6. Runia 1986, 411.

7. Reese 1970, 3. For two examples, cf. *Wis.* 11:17 with Pl. *Ti.* 50D–51A, and cf. *Wis.* 7:17–18 with Pl. *Ti.* 57C; see Winston 1971 and J. Laporte in Wilken 1975, 103–41.

8. Gager 1972, 32 n. 23, with bibliography; Bickerman 1976, 171; see the materials collected in Marcus 1945.

9. Reale 1979, 247–87; see the summary by Henry Chadwick in Armstrong 1967, 133–57.

10. Phil. *Opif.* 89.

11. Phil. *Opif.* 127, 104.

12. Phil. *Opif.* 128.

13. Phil. *Opif.* 119, 133; Phil. *Opif.* 21, quoting Pl. *Ti.* 29E.

Philo summarized the cosmogony (κοσμοποιία) of *Genesis* in five points, which were "most beautiful and best of all" [κάλλιστα καὶ πάντων ἄριστα],[14] and which may be used here to describe the counterpoint between *Timaeus* and *Genesis* in Alexandria, "an interpretation of Genesis in terms of the *Timaeus*—not in terms of the *Timaeus* as it is written, but rather in terms of the *Timaeus* as it was understood by Philo" and other Alexandrian Jews.[15]

The God of Moses as the ὁ ὤν of Plato

In its polemic against idolatry, *Wisdom* issued a scathing denunciation of the "born fools" who, "from the good before their eyes could not learn him who is [τὸν ὄντα]."[16] But in Alexandria this way of speaking about God and Being—fraught with the speculations of *Timaeus* about the fundamental difference between the mere "Becoming" [γένεσις] of the world perceptible to the senses, ὁ κόσμος αἰσθητός, and the genuine "Being" [οὐσία] of the world apprehensible only to the mind, ὁ κόσμος νοητός[17]—had been put into the service of speaking about the God of Israel, who in the call to Moses had identified himself by declaring, first, "I am the God of your father, the God of Abraham, Isaac, and Jacob," and, second, according to the Septuagint, Ἐγώ εἰμι ὁ ὤν.[18] Nevertheless, Philo took it on himself to reverse this order: "God replied [to Moses]: 'First tell them that Ἐγώ εἰμι ὁ ὤν'"; this would teach that there was a difference between the One who was true being and all those who were not and would make it clear that "no name at all can properly be used of Me, to whom alone existence belongs."[19] Only after delivering this strictly accurate designation was Moses to go on, as a concession to human weakness, to identify ὁ ὤν also as "the God of the three men whose names express their virtue [ἀρετή]," specifically the virtue of "wisdom" [σοφία], which in Abraham had come from "teaching," in Isaac was "self-learnt," and in Jacob had come from "practice" [δι' ἀσκήσεως].[20] That reversal of order in Philo's version of the history of Moses affords an insight into the Alexandrian interpretation of the history of the creation of the universe as

14. Phil. *Opif.* 170–71.
15. Wolfson 1947, 1:307.
16. *Wis.* 13:1.
17. Pl. *Ti.* 29C.
18. *Ex.* 3:7, 14.
19. Phil. *V. Mos.* 1.75; Nikiprowetzky 1977, 58–62.
20. Phil. *V. Mos.* 1.76; Phil. *Congr.* 35–36.

narrated by Moses in *Genesis* and by Plato in *Timaeus,* in which the Creator God of Moses was the ὁ ὢν of Plato.

Prominent in this Alexandrian interpretation was an overriding insistence on the mysteries of "God's hidden plan" [μυστήρια θεοῦ]²¹ and the transcendence of the Creator God. The "active cause" of all reality was "the perfectly pure and unsullied Mind of the universe," which was "transcendent" [κρείττων] not only over material things but over "virtue" [ἀρετή], over "precise scientific knowledge" [ἐπιστήμη], and even over "the Good itself and the Beautiful itself" [αὐτὸ τὸ ἀγαθὸν καὶ αὐτὸ τὸ καλόν].²² All of these were "in his hand," because God the Creator did not stand in need of his creatures, on which he bestowed "powers but not independence."²³ The "authority" and power of kings came from the sovereignty of the Most High.²⁴ Yet precisely because it was beyond the capacity of any writer "in verse or prose" to give an adequate treatment of "the beauty of the ideas embodied in this account of the creation of the world," which transcended affirmation in speech, it was necessary to be "venturesome."²⁵ That apophatic requirement called for a method of thinking and speaking about the Creator "by analogy" [ἀναλόγως], a method that would, "by a natural steppingstone" [κατὰ μετάβασιν], derive a "conception of the Uncreated and Eternal, the invisible Charioteer who guides in safety the whole universe."²⁶ The human mind, which on its own would never have ventured "to grasp the nature of God" [ἀντιλαβέσθαι θεοῦ φύσεως], could now reach out in an attempt to do so, because God "stamped" [ἐτύπωσε] it with the impress of "the powers that are within the scope of its understanding."²⁷

"In the beginning God," *Genesis* insisted: God had ordered heaven after ordering earth, "to make clear beyond all doubt the mighty sway of His sovereign power" [εἰς ἔνδειξιν ἐναργεστάτην κράτους ἀρχῆς].²⁸ Because of *Genesis,* any such method of analogy and comparison was obliged to draw a sharp distinction between Creator and creature and to do so even when it was speaking in the vocabulary of *Timaeus* about the immanent activity of the Creator in the creation. One way to do this was

---

21. *Wis.* 2:22.
22. Phil. *Opif.* 8.
23. *Wis.* 7:16; Phil. *Opif.* 46.
24. *Wis.* 6:3.
25. Phil. *Opif.* 4–5.
26. *Wis.* 13:5; Phil. *Decal.* 60.
27. Phil. *Leg. all.* 1.38.
28. *Gn.* 1:1; Phil. *Opif.* 45.

to distinguish, among "the things which come into being," between those things that "come into being both by God's power and through God's agency" [ὑπὸ θεοῦ γίνεται καὶ δι' αὐτοῦ] and those that "come into being by God's power but not by His agency." The most excellent things were those that were made both "by" [ὑπό] and "through" [διά] God, although all things in "heaven and earth" were under "the sway of His sovereign power" even when they were not by His agency.[29] Thus "the cosmogonic power" [ἡ δύναμις κοσμοποιητική] was equated with a power "that has as its source nothing less than true goodness" [τὸ πρὸς ἀλήθειαν ἀγαθόν],[30] an equation that was not made in the cosmogonic account of Genesis, but that, once made, could be seen as the central meaning of that account. For the God of Moses was "a God who loves to give good things."[31]

For that very reason, one of the central themes of the cosmogony of Timaeus could now be put into the service of the cosmogony of Genesis. Genesis had not spoken about the underlying motive for the creation: it happened simply because God willed it, no questions asked. But according to Timaeus, the Demiurge "was good, and . . . being free from jealousy, desired that all things should be as like himself as they could be."[32] David Runia has noted that in "an event of enormous significance in the history of ideas," Philo became "the first thinker to associate the goodness of Plato's demiurge with the Judaeo-Christian conception of God the creator."[33] As Philo put the counterpoint between the two cosmogonies concerning creation, "its cause is God" (both Timaeus and Genesis), "its material the four elements" (Timaeus), "its instrument the word of God" (Genesis); and "the final cause of the building is the goodness of the architect" (Timaeus read into Genesis).[34] Specifically, Philo noted that goodness was an attribute of the God of Moses, whom the word from the burning bush equated with the ὁ ὤν of Plato: "Those who have studied more deeply than others the laws of Moses and who examine their contents with all possible minuteness maintain that God . . . did not begrudge [οὐδὲ ἐφθόνησεν]"[35] (the verb Philo uses corresponds to Plato's noun in Timaeus, φθόνος). Quoting Timaeus for the exegesis of Genesis, Philo declared: "Should one conceive a wish to search for the cause, for the sake

---

29. Phil. Leg. all. 1.41; Phil. Opif. 45.
30. Phil. Opif. 21.
31. Phil. Leg. all. 1.34.
32. Pl. Ti. 29E (Jowett).
33. Runia 1986, 135.
34. Phil. Cher. 127; see Bousset 1915, 25–28.
35. Phil. Opif. 77.

of which this whole was created [τόδε τὸ πᾶν ἐδημιουργεῖτο], it seems to me that he would not be wrong in saying, what indeed one of the men of old did say, that the Father and Maker of all is good; and because of this He grudged not a share in his own excellent nature [φύσεως οὐκ ἐφθόνησεν οὐσίᾳ]."[36] Here Philo the monotheist was equating with the ὁ ὤν of Plato not only the Creator God of Moses but the Creator Demiurge of Plato.

The God and Father of the Universe as One

That equating was made necessary and possible by the second of Philo's axioms: "That God is one" [ὅτι θεὸς εἷς ἐστι]; and again, "That He that really IS is One" [ὅτι εἷς ὁ ὤν ὄντως ἐστι].[37] In his exposition of the First Commandment, he elaborated on this axiom and its corollary rejection of polytheism: "Let us, then, engrave deep in our hearts this as the first and most sacred of commandments, to acknowledge and honour one God Who is above all, and let the idea that gods are many never even reach the ears of the man whose rule of life is to seek for truth in purity and guilelessness."[38] By this commandment God had "called upon men to honour Him that truly is."[39] Such an unambiguous adherence to the monotheism of the Pentateuch makes it all the more curious "that Philo never directly quotes in support of it that classical scriptural proof-text," the Shema of *Deuteronomy* 6:4. "It is probably," Harry Wolfson suggests, "because this principle was so commonly well known among those of his contemporaries to whom he addressed himself in his works," for "in Palestine this belief in the unity of God constituted a principle of faith which was twice daily confessed by the recitation" of the Shema, and "undoubtedly the same confession of the belief in the unity of God was also followed twice daily by Hellenistic Jews" (Wolfson provides no documentation for this suggestion).[40] The criticism of Greek polytheism was a frequently recurring theme in the philosophy of Athens as well as in the religion of Jerusalem, as the sarcasm of *Timaeus* made clear.[41] One such sarcastic criticism appeared in *Wisdom*, with a parallel in *Isaiah*, about the woodcutter who felled a tree, worked some of its wood into an object useful for daily life, burned some of it to cook a meal, and then made "one

---

36. Phil. *Opif.* 21; see Brisson 1974, 155 n. 1.
37. Phil. *Opif.* 171–72.
38. Phil. *Decal.* 65.
39. Phil. *Decal.* 81.
40. Wolfson 1947, 2:95.
41. Pl. *Ti.* 40D–E.

useless piece, crooked and full of knots," into a god.[42] Idolatry, because of the intellectual and moral confusion it caused, was "the beginning, the cause, and the end of every evil" and "the beginning of immorality."[43] Opposite though they seemed, such polytheism and atheism were two sides of the same denial of monotheism.[44] Biblical monotheism, the doctrine that "there is only one ruler and governor and king, to whom alone it is granted to govern and to arrange the universe," could find support in Homer as quoted by Aristotle: "The rule of many is not good; one ruler let there be."[45] If that was true of the polis, it "could be said with more justice of the world and of God than of cities and men. For being one it must needs have one maker and father and master."[46]

As that quotation suggests, the formula of *Timaeus*, "Maker and Father of this Universe,"[47] could, by the equation of the Creator God of *Genesis* with the Creator Demiurge of *Timaeus*, be put into the service of Mosaic monotheism. The metaphor of God as Father, which was to be so prominent in the teaching of Jesus and in the Christian doctrine of the Trinity, was not unknown in the Hebrew Bible, where God was the Father of Israel, the Father and protector of the orphan;[48] only by inference, however, was *Father* to be synonymous with *Creator*, even for the New Testament, although in the various Christian creeds of antiquity that identification became standard, as in the opening formula of the Niceno-Constantinopolitan Creed, Πιστεύομεν εἰς ἕνα θεὸν πατέρα παντοκράτορα.[49] In Alexandrian Judaism, the "boast that God is his father"[50] was effortlessly extended to the entire cosmos, so that it was taken as the intended meaning of the cosmogony of *Genesis* that God "is not a mere artificer, but also Father of the things that are coming into being" [οὐ τεχνίτης μόνον ἀλλὰ καὶ πατὴρ ὢν τῶν γινομένων].[51] Those words of Philo resonated across much of the corpus of his works. Particularly in the middle section of *De opificio mundi*, this theme recurred often. Directly from the *Timaeus* came its formula ὁ ποιητὴς καὶ πατήρ,[52] which gave

42. *Wis.* 13:11–19; *Is.* 44:13–17.
43. *Wis.* 14:27, 12.
44. Phil. *Migr.* 69.
45. Hom. *Il.* 2.204; Arist. *Met.* Λ.1076a5.
46. Phil. *Conf.* 170.
47. Pl. *Ti.* 28C.
48. For example, *Ps.* 68:5 and *Is.* 64:8.
49. Tanner-Alberigo, 1:24.
50. *Wis.* 2:16.
51. Phil. *Leg. all.* 1.18.
52. Phil. *Opif.* 77, a verbatim quotation of the formula from Pl. *Ti.* 28C.

content to other formulas: τὸν πατέρα τῶν ὅλων; τῷ δὴ πάντων πατρὶ θεῷ; γεννήσας αὐτὸν [τὸν ἄνθρωπον] ὁ πατήρ; ὁ πατήρ; ἐκ τοῦ πατρὸς καὶ ἡγεμόνος τῶν πάντων; τοῦ πατρὸς καὶ βασιλέως.[53]

In addition to the novelty of describing the Creator as Father, what set this Alexandrian version of the doctrine of creation apart from most biblical monotheism was the participation of other beings in the divine act of creation. Philo made it clear that God had "no counselor to help Him [οὐδενὶ παρακλήτῳ], for who was there beside Him?"[54] Nevertheless, the cosmogony of *Genesis* had, at the crucial point of the creation of the human race, resorted to a plural: "Let *us* make man" [Ποιήσωμεν ἄνθρωπον].[55] Why should such a plural have appeared at all, and why in this particular context? "Can it be," Philo asked himself, "that He to whom all things are subject is in need of anyone whatever? Or can it be that when He made the heaven and the earth and the seas, he required no one to be his fellow-worker, yet was unable apart from the co-operation of others by His own unaided power to fashion a creature so puny and perishable as man?"[56] His conjectural answer was that the human soul alone was "susceptible of conceptions of evil things and good things"; when the soul followed the good things, that obedience to good could be attributed to "God the universal Ruler as their Source," whereas human disobedience could be attributed to "others from the number of His subordinates," who "imitated" the action of the Creator.[57] This read into *Genesis* the statement of *Timaeus* that the lesser deities, "imitating" [μιμούμενοι] the Demiurge, "received from him the immortal principle of the soul, and around this they proceeded to fashion a mortal body," in which there would be "a soul of another nature," subject to pleasure and pain.[58]

Yet even Philo seemed to recognize that this explanation of the plural was less than satisfactory; both he and *Wisdom* posited the presence of a distinct and quasi-hypostatic reality in the act of creation—Logos for Philo, Sophia for *Wisdom*—though without directly connecting it to *Genesis* 1:26 as the unidentified addressee of "Let us make." Justification for the first of these concepts, Philo's Logos, came from the repeated use in the *Genesis* cosmogony of the phrase "And God said" as the instrument (or agent) of creation, and from the repeated use in the *Timaeus* cos-

---

53. Phil. *Opif.* 72, 74, 84, 89, 135, 144.
54. Phil. *Opif.* 23.
55. *Gn.* 1:26.
56. Phil. *Opif.* 72.
57. Phil. *Fug.* 68–70; Phil. *Opif.* 73–75.
58. Pl. *Ti.* 69C–D; Wolfson 1947, 1:387.

mogony of Reason as the divine element both in the cosmos and in man; the Greek word λόγος, meaning both "word" and "reason," was especially suitable as a bridge between these two. The justification for the second concept, Sophia in *Wisdom,* was above all the personification of wisdom in the canonical *Proverbs,* likewise attributed to Solomon. On that basis, as David Winston has put it, the author of *Wisdom* "is saying in effect that Wisdom is essentially synonymous with the Divine Mind, and thus represents the creative agent of the Deity. The similarity of this conception with Philo's Logos doctrine is unmistakable."[59]

In Philo's *De opificio mundi,* with monotheism as a major theme, the doctrine of the Logos, coming right after the statement that God had no παράκλητος in creation, was an attempt to provide a principle of mediation (which *Timaeus* did and *Genesis* needed) while preserving monotheism (which *Genesis* did and *Timaeus* needed).[60] In defense of his juxtaposed reading of the two texts, Philo insisted: "This doctrine comes from Moses, not from me" [τὸ δὲ δόγμα τοῦτο Μωυσέως ἐστίν, οὐκ ἐμόν]. But the δόγμα he was defending as authentically Mosaic was this: "The cosmos that is apprehensible only by the mind is nothing else than the Logos of God when He [God] was already engaged in the act of creating the cosmos" [τὸν νοητὸν κόσμον εἶναι . . . θεοῦ λόγου ἤδη κοσμοποιοῦν-τος]. Its fundamental presupposition was, then, the distinctly non-Mosaic, or at any rate extra-Mosaic, distinction between "the cosmos that is apprehensible only to the mind" and "the cosmos that is perceptible to the senses."[61] And the proof that this was genuinely Mosaic was the statement of *Genesis* that man was created "after the image of God," which was by extension applied to the entire world of the senses, now seen as the image of the world of the mind, which was equated with the Logos of God.[62] The Timaean and generally Platonic metaphor of the design that preexisted in the mind of the architect before it became a city was applied to the Logos of God as the one who "provided cosmic order [διακοσμήσαντα] to that cosmos which consisted of ideas [ὁ ἐκ τῶν ἰδεῶν κόσμος]."[63] This Logos transcended all the beauties of the world of perception, being "not only adorned with beauty, but Himself in very truth

---

59. On this at least, Winston (1979, 194 n. 4), and Wolfson (1947, 1:255), are in agreement.

60. See Colpe 1979; Tobin 1983, 44–48.

61. Farandos 1976, 297–306, with diagram; Vogel 1985, 8–12.

62. Phil. *Opif.* 24–25. Jervell 1960, 52–70; Winden 1983.

63. Phil. *Opif.* 20; cf. Pl. *Ti.* 77C.

beauty's fairest adornment."[64] It was to the human soul and logos that "the holy Logos" bore a special relation.[65] That was clear from the Mosaic doctrine of the image of God, an image whose "pattern" [παράδειγμα] was found not in any other creature but in the divine Logos, of which the first man "was made an image and copy" [ἀπεικόνισμα καὶ μίμημα].[66] His descendants also participated "faintly" in the image of the Logos "as far as their mind was concerned."[67]

Many of the qualities thus attributed to the divine Logos were likewise predicated of the divine Sophia. Philo himself made this equation: "The Wisdom of God . . . is the Reason of God [τῆς τοῦ θεοῦ σοφίας. ἡ δέ ἐστιν ὁ θεοῦ λόγος]."[68] Wisdom, he explained, was "many-named" [πολυώνυμος], being called, among other things, "beginning" [ἀρχή], "image" [εἰκών], and "vision of God" [ὅρασις θεοῦ]; like Logos, moreover, Sophia existed both as a "heavenly" archetype and as an "earthly" copy.[69] The author of *Wisdom* took up the theme of her "many names," describing her or the "spirit" [πνεῦμα] in her, to which she seemed to be assimilated later,[70] "in a series of twenty-one (7 × 3) epithets, borrowed largely from Greek philosophy" and paralleled in other Near Eastern texts.[71] Among these epithets was μονογενές, which appeared at the conclusion of the *Timaeus*.[72] Another of the epithets for Sophia was φιλάνθρωπος, which had already been applied to her at the beginning of *Wisdom*.[73] The same attribute belonged, according to Philo, also to God, who was φιλάρετος καὶ φιλόκαλος καὶ προσέτι φιλάνθρωπος.[74] The relation of Sophia to God, therefore, was complex and subtle. Sophia was "the radiance that streams from everlasting light, the flawless mirror of the active power of God, and the image of his goodness" [ἀπαύγασμα φωτὸς ἀιδίου καὶ ἔσοπτρον ἀκηλίδωτον τῆς τοῦ θεοῦ ἐνεργείας καὶ εἰκὼν τῆς ἀγαθότητος αὐτοῦ];[75] the last of these attributes was an important point of convergence between *Timaeus* and *Genesis*.[76]

---

64. Phil. *Opif.* 139.
65. Phil. *Leg. all.* 1.16.
66. Phil. *Opif.* 139; Mack 1972, 36–41.
67. Phil. *Opif.* 145–46.
68. Phil. *Leg. all.* 1.65. See Früchtel 1968, 172–78.
69. Phil. *Leg. all.* 1.43.
70. *Wis.* 9:17.
71. *Wis.* 7:22–24; Winston 1979, 178–83.
72. Pl. *Ti.* 92C.
73. *Wis.* 1:6.
74. Phil. *Opif.* 81.
75. *Wis.* 7:26.
76. Pl. *Ti.* 29B; *Gn.* 1:26–27; Phil. *Opif.* 25.

Another point of convergence was the title τεχνίτης, which for Philo was a title for God although it was overshadowed by the title πατὴρ τῶν γινομένων, and which in *Wisdom* was a title for Sophia.[77]

γενητὸς ὁ κόσμος

The problem of the apparent contradiction between the monotheistic language of *Genesis* and the function of such auxiliary agents as Logos and Sophia (and Pneuma) in Philo and *Wisdom*, whatever their relation to the Demiurge of *Timaeus* may have been, came to a focus in the doctrine of creation.[78] Philo set it down as his third summary point: " . . . that the cosmos has come into being [γενητὸς ὁ κόσμος]. This because of those who think that it is without beginning and eternal [ἀγένητον καὶ ἀΐδιον], who thus assign to God no superiority at all."[79] Any philosophical treatment of cosmogony had to confront the scientific issue of the constituent elements of the cosmos. The statement in *Wisdom* about God's "almighty hand, which created the world out of formless matter" [κτίσασα τὸν κόσμον ἐξ ἀμόρφου ὕλης], seemed to employ the language of the *Timaeus*, requiring harmonization with biblical teaching.[80] Plato's *Timaeus* was, together with *Theaetetus*, where that issue had been systematically formulated on the basis of earlier theories.[81] All four of these "elements στοιχεῖα" did receive some kind of mention in the course of the first three verses of *Genesis*, without being identified by any such term. But they were identified as such with the technical term στοιχεῖα both by Philo and in *Wisdom*. It seemed to be a quotation of the formula of *Timaeus*, τὴν ἑκατέρου τῶν στοιχείων αἰτιατέον ξυστασιν, when the *Book of Wisdom* spoke of εἰδέναι ὑστασιν κόσμου καὶ ἐνέργειαν στοιχείων.[82] Sometimes, even with that technical term, all four elements did not appear at the same time.[83] It was uniquely human, according to Philo, to share in all four elements and to be at home in any of them.[84]

Conversely, a review of the writings of Moses, chiefly in *Genesis* but also elsewhere in the Pentateuch, led to significant correctives on these Timaean allusions. In contrast to "other philosophers," who called all

77. Phil. *Leg. all.* 1.18; *Wis.* 7:21, 8:6.
78. Runia 1986, 7–31.
79. Phil. *Opif.* 171.
80. *Wis.* 11:17; Pl. *Ti.* 50D–51A; Reale 1979, 273–81.
81. Pl. *Ti.* 31B, 32B, 48B; Pl. *Tht.* 201E.
82. Pl. *Ti.* 57C; *Wis.* 7:17.
83. *Wis.* 13:2; Phil. *Opif.* 38, 84.
84. Phil. *Opif.* 147.

water indiscriminately ἕν στοιχεῖον . . . τῶν τεττάρων, ἐξ ὧν ὁ κόσμος ἐδημιουργήθη, Moses in *Genesis* distinguished between freshwater and saltwater.[85] The history of the Exodus from Egypt, also celebrated by the second half of *Wisdom* as evidence of divine power and providence, provided Philo with a basis for describing how the God of Israel had demonstrated "the mightiness of the sovereignty which He holds" by employing all four elements against Israel's enemies. Thus the almighty Creator "turned into instruments for the perdition of the impious" the elements that originally "He shaped in His saving goodness to create the universe."[86] *Wisdom* described how "the elements combined among themselves in different ways" [τὰ στοιχεῖα μεθαρμοζόμενα] in the Exodus.[87] One of the four provided Philo with another way of employing the cosmogony of *Genesis* to differentiate his views from the cosmogony of *Timaeus*. Plato had subsumed his discussion of light under the category of fire.[88] But light had no such subordinate position in the cosmogony of *Genesis,* where it was the first of all creatures, inducted with the first magisterial "And God said" and greeted by God's first καλόν.[89] The primeval light, perceptible only to the mind, Philo said, was "beautiful pre-eminently" [ὑπερβαλλόντως καλόν], for it was "an image of the Divine Logos" [θείου λόγου εἰκών]. "It would not be amiss," he continued, to term it "all-brightness" [παναύγεια], because from it all the lights perceived by the senses in heaven and on earth derived "the light befitting each of them" [τὰ πρέποντα φέγγη].[90] And after God had on the first day kindled this "φῶς νοητόν, which preceded the sun's creation," this latter being an event reserved for the fourth day, "darkness its adversary withdrew." Thus a distinction of *Timaeus* made it possible for Philo as interpreter of *Genesis* to account for the puzzling hiatus between the creation of light on the first day and the creation of the sun on the fourth.

Philo's celebration of the divine fiat in *Genesis,* as well as his subordination of the στοιχεῖα of *Timaeus* to the divine "mightiness of the sovereignty" of a God who had also fashioned those same elements at the creation of the universe and could change them all whenever he pleased,[91] highlighted an even more fundamental difference:

---

85. Phil. *Opif.* 131.
86. *Wis.* 10:15–19:22; Phil. *V. Mos.* 1.96.
87. *Wis.* 19:18.
88. Pl. *Ti.* 45B–C.
89. *Gn.* 1:3–4.
90. Phil. *Opif.* 30–31.
91. Phil. *V. Mos.* 1.96.

Three times in the account of the act of creation, Plato emphasizes that the god *willed,* not (note well!) that the cosmos should or should not come into being, but that it be as good as possible (29e3, 30a2, d3). In his commentary on the creational account Philo eagerly takes over the notion of God's will, but, in contrast to Plato, applies it to the actual decision to create the cosmos. God *willed* to create this visible cosmos (*Opif.* 16 βουληθεὶς τὸν ὁρατὸν κόσμον τουτονὶ δημιουργῆσαι).[92]

This emphasis on the divine will and command to create the cosmos contrasts with the language of *Timaeus* about the process by which the Demiurge "led it into order from disorder" [εἰς τάξιν αὐτὸ ἤγαγεν ἐκ τῆς ἀταξίας] and about "persuasion" [πείθειν] as his means of creation.[93] "How could anything have continued in existence," *Wisdom* asked, "had it not been your will? How could it have endured unless called into being by you?"[94] For example, when God commanded, "Let the earth bring forth living creatures, according to their various kinds," the response to the command was immediate: "The earth forthwith puts forth, as it was bidden."[95]

With the distinction of *Timaeus* between κόσμος νοητός and κόσμος αἰσθητός, Philo was able to superimpose on the cosmogony of *Genesis*—or to find in it, as he would have preferred to say—an entire systematic theory of pattern and copy derived from the cosmogony of *Timaeus* and based on the presupposition that "God, being God, assumed that a beautiful copy [μίμημα καλόν] would never be produced apart from a beautiful pattern [παράδειγμα καλόν]." Therefore there were two distinct creations, of the κόσμος νοητός first, and then of the κόσμος αἰσθητός, which God made as "the very image" [ἀπεικόνισμα] of the first.[96] What was described in the opening words of the Bible was the creation of the invisible, archetypal "heaven and earth," the κόσμος νοητός.[97] Before a particular and individual mind there had to have existed "an idea, as an archetype and pattern of it" [τις ἰδέα, ὡς ἂν ἀρχέτυπος καὶ παράδειγμα τούτου].[98] The whole creation was "a copy of the divine image" [μίμημα

92. Runia 1986, 139.
93. Pl. *Ti.* 30A, 48A.
94. *Wis.* 11:25.
95. *Gn.* 1:24; Phil. *Opif.* 64.
96. Phil. *Opif.* 16.
97. Phil. *Opif.* 29.
98. Phil. *Leg. all.* 1.22.

θείας εἰκόνος].⁹⁹ From *Timaeus* it could be learned that the Creator of *Genesis* was like an architect.¹⁰⁰ That implied, for example, that Solomon, in building his temple, was constructing "a copy [μίμημα] of the sacred tabernacle prepared by [God] from the beginning."¹⁰¹ But the most brilliant application of the Timaean distinction to the creation story of *Genesis* enabled Philo to solve the vexing problem of the two versions of the creation of man by applying to it the double creation, first of the immortal soul and then of the mortal body, posited in *Timaeus:*¹⁰² the man formed of clay in the second version (*Gn.* 2:7) was "perceptible to the senses" [αἰσθητός], whereas the man created after the image of God in the first version was "apprehensible only to the mind [νοητός], neither male nor female, by nature incorruptible," as was the God in whose image that man was created.¹⁰³ That was why the text said that after receiving the breath of the divine life, he not only received but "*became* a living soul."¹⁰⁴

Both the pattern and the copy were the work of the Almighty Creator, who was not confined to time; for "the cosmos was not made in time, but time was formed by means of the cosmos," and time "was not before there was a cosmos."¹⁰⁵ From this it followed that God made "the commands which He issues together with the thought behind them," both the pattern and the copy "simultaneously."¹⁰⁶ But the problem that according to the cosmogony in *Genesis* light was created on the first day and the sun on the fourth was one illustration of the exegetical obligation to deal with "the chain of sequence" [ὁ τῆς ἀκουλουθίας εἱρμός] of the "bringing in of life" [ζῳογονία] in the hexaemeron.¹⁰⁷ Part of the answer was numerological: like Plato before him and Augustine after him, Philo found six to be "the first perfect number" because it was the sum of its constituent parts, one, two, and three.¹⁰⁸ But the most important reason for the use of a sequence that seemed to be, but was not, chronological was "the necessity of order [ἡ τάξις]."¹⁰⁹ This he defined in general as "a series of things going on before and following after, in due sequence, a sequence

---

99. Phil. *Opif.* 25.
100. Phil. *Opif.* 17–18.
101. *Wis.* 9:8.
102. Pl. *Ti.* 69C.
103. Phil. *Opif.* 134.
104. Phil. *Leg. all.* 1.31–32.
105. Phil. *Leg. all.* 1.2; Phil. *Opif.* 26. See Baltes 1976, 32–38.
106. Phil. *Opif.* 13.
107. Phil. *Opif.* 65.
108. Phil. *Opif.* 13; Pl. *Resp.* 8.546B; Aug. *Civ.* 11.30. See Ladner 1959, 212–22.
109. Phil. *Opif.* 67.

which, though not seen in the finished product, yet exists in the designs of the contrivers"; and it had to be "an attribute of all that came into existence in fair beauty, for beauty is absent where there is disorder."[110] The division of the simultaneous creation into six days, "to each of which He assigned some of the portions of the whole, not including, however, the first day, which He does not even call 'first' [πρώτη], lest it should be reckoned with the others, but naming it 'one' [μία],"[111] suited precisely the definition of creation in *Timaeus* as the process by which the Demiurge "led it into order from disorder."[112] And the name for what he led into order was "cosmos."

One Demiurge and One Cosmos

The fourth of Philo's summary axioms about creation was also the longest: ". . . that the world [κόσμος] too is one as well as its Maker [δημιουργός], who made His work like Himself in its uniqueness [κατὰ τὴν μόνωσιν], who used up for the creation [γένεσις] of the whole all the material that exists; for it would not have been a whole had it not been formed and consisted of parts that were wholes. For there are those who suppose that there are more worlds than one, while some think that they are infinite in number. Such men are themselves in very deed infinitely lacking in knowledge of things which it is right good to know."[113] For Philo, the oneness of the cosmos was a corollary of the oneness of God the Creator, and the case for the former was dependent on the case for the latter, to which both *Timaeus* and *Genesis* had contributed. The question itself came directly from *Timaeus:* "Are we right in saying that there is one world [ἕνα οὐρανόν], or that they are many and infinite? There must be one only if the created copy is to accord with the original."[114] Paradoxical though it might have seemed to some Middle Platonic readers of *Timaeus* as well as to certain Stoics, the oneness of God the Creator and the oneness of the cosmos were both grounded not in any identification of God with the cosmos but in the fundamental ontological distinction between Creator and creature. It was the inspired insight of "the great Moses" to recognize that distinction, which *Wisdom* formulated with special sharpness.[115] The alternative to atheism was not pantheism but

110. Phil. *Opif.* 28.
111. Phil. *Opif.* 15, 35; *Gn.* 1:5 LXX.
112. Pl. *Ti.* 30A.
113. Phil. *Opif.* 171.
114. Pl. *Ti.* 31A (Jowett).
115. Phil. *Opif.* 12; *Wis.* 13:1–5.

divine transcendence: because the transcendent God was one, it was possible for the creation to be one, "like Him in its oneness."

Nevertheless, the very device from *Timaeus* that helped make sense of the double creation of man in *Genesis* appeared to introduce a fundamental metaphysical cleavage into the doctrine of man as the crown of creation and thus, by extension, into the entire doctrine of creation. Philo attributed to Moses the principle that "everything that is perceptible to the senses is subject to becoming and to constant change," by contrast with "that which is invisible and apprehensible only to the mind."[116] First the distinction between the world perceived by the mind and the world perceived by the senses, and then the unity between them, were set forth in the single formula of *Genesis:* "And the heaven and the earth and all their cosmos were completed" [Καὶ συνετελέσθησαν ὁ οὐρανὸς καὶ ἡ γῆ καὶ πᾶς ὁ κόσμος αὐτῶν].[117] *Heaven* in this sentence meant "mind, since heaven is the abode of natures discerned only by mind." *Earth* referred to "sense-perception, because sense-perception possesses a composition of a more earthly and body-like sort." But *cosmos* embraced them both, the incorporeal things of the mind and the corporeal things of the bodily senses, which therefore could be seen as "one" in the single cosmos of the one God.[118] That comprehensive vision of "the entire cosmos" was symbolically set forth on the liturgical robes of the high priest Aaron.[119]

Both the distinction and the unity between νοῦς and αἴσθησις became the basis for dealing with the unity of the human race, specifically the relation between man and woman in creation, an issue on which both *Timaeus* and *Genesis* had given problematical answers.[120] In a retrospective interpretation of the account of creation in the light of the subsequent account of the fall of Adam and Eve, Philo once more invoked the distinction between νοῦς and αἴσθησις: "pleasure" [ἡδονή] (a feminine noun in Greek), as symbolized by the serpent, "does not venture to bring her wiles and deceptions to bear on the man, but on the woman, and by her means on him." This was because νοῦς (masculine in Greek) represented man, and αἴσθησις (feminine) represented woman; pleasure attacks the senses first, and then through them "it cheats even the sovereign mind itself."[121] But just as "cosmos" in the Septuagint of *Genesis* 2:1 represented the

---

116. Phil. *Opif.* 12.
117. *Gn.* 2:1.
118. Phil. *Leg. all.* 1.1.
119. *Wis.* 18:24; Bousset 1915, 37–40.
120. Pl. *Ti.* 90E; *Gn.* 2:18–25.
121. Phil. *Opif.* 165.

unity of heaven and earth, and therefore also the unity between τὸ νοητόν and τὸ αἰσθητόν, so, despite the identification of νοῦς with the masculine and αἴσθησις with the feminine, the first created human being, the one made in accordance with the image of God, was in fact "neither male nor female."[122] In this divine image the differences among human beings, not only between male and female but other differences as well, could be transcended.[123] For Philo did not follow *Timaeus* and describe women as men undergoing punishment; rather he followed *Genesis,* attributing the creation of both male and female to God and declaring that "woman, too, was made" by the Creator.[124]

Similarly, the unity of the cosmos as grounded in the unity of its Creator made possible a sense not only of the distinction but also of the kinship between man and the other animals. Continuing its explanation of woman, *Timaeus* had interpreted the various species of animals, too, as several levels of punishment inflicted on human beings.[125] But on this issue Philo followed *Genesis,* asserting that the Creator "took in hand to form the races of mortal creatures" [τὰ θνητὰ γένη ζωοπλαστεῖν ἐνεχεί-ρει].[126] The repeated language of the Septuagint about animals possessing a ψύχη—as when God commanded the seas, !Ἐξαγαγέτω τὰ ὕδατα ἑρπετὰ ψυχῶν ζωσῶν, and then the land, !Ἐξαγαγέτω ἡ γῆ ψυχὴν ζῶσαν—enabled Philo to distinguish creatures that were ἔμψυχα from those that did not possess a soul of any kind, on the basis that beings with a ψύχη were also endowed with the ability of sense perception (αἴσθησις).[127] This included not only animals of sea and land but also man, who was distinct from all others and unique in his relation to God by virtue of having a ψύχη that was "mind *par excellence*"[128] and that connected him to the κόσμος νοητός, but who, by what he shared with the animals, participated in the κόσμος αἰσθητός as well. Ultimately, the oneness of the cosmos could be said to be guaranteed by the same factor that seemed to make the oneness of the Creator problematical in Hellenistic Judaism, the presence of Logos and/or Sophia. The arrangement of heaven, like that of earth, was "in varied beauty."[129] But despite the seemingly infinite variety of these crea-

122. Phil. *Leg. all.* 1.1; Phil. *Opif.* 134.
123. Phil. *Leg. all.* 3.96.
124. Phil. *Opif.* 151; Pl. *Ti.* 90E.
125. Pl. *Ti.* 91E–92C.
126. Phil. *Opif.* 62.
127. *Gn.* 1:20, 24; Phil. *Opif.* 62.
128. Phil. *Opif.* 66.
129. Phil. *Opif.* 45.

tures, it remained true that God had "made them all by the instrumentality of the Logos."[130] The Logos was "all-healing."[131] Behind all the particularities of the world perceptible to the senses were the Ideas apprehensible only to the mind, but behind and before both of them was "the archetypal model, the Idea of Ideas, the Logos of God" [τὸ παράδειγμα, ἀρχέτυπος ἰδέα τῶν ἰδεῶν ὁ θεοῦ λόγος].[132] Thus the Logos provided the unity of the Ideas with one another, which in turn united the objects of sense.

Divine Providence in the Cosmos

"The fifth lesson that Moses teaches us," Philo summarized, "is that God exerts his providence for the benefit of the cosmos."[133] The term πρόνοια in the sense of divine providence did not occur in any of the translations from Hebrew in the Septuagint (although the concept was fundamental, for example, in the history of the Exodus). But it did occur in *Timaeus,* in the important statement of its theme: "On this wise, using the language of probability, we may say that the world came into being—a living creature truly endowed with soul and intelligence by the providence of God [διὰ τὴν τοῦ θεοῦ πρόνοιαν]."[134] And it did occur, for the first time in the Greek version of the Bible, in *Wisdom:* "Your providence, Father, is the pilot" [ἡ δὲ σή, πάτερ, διακυβερνᾷ πρόνοια]; "fugitives from eternal providence."[135] The idea, though not the word, was repeated in such prayers as "You are just and you order all things [τὰ πάντα] justly," as well as in the review of the actions of the divine Sophia in the history of Israel.[136] The alternative to the doctrine of providence, Philo declared, was "a worthless and baleful doctrine," which would "introduce anarchy in the cosmos."[137] If the one God was indeed "Father and Maker," it logically followed that by his providence he would care for what he had made.[138] Philo provided the fundamental presupposition for the doctrine of providence when—taking advantage of the Septuagint translation, which said that God "caused to rest" [κατέπαυσεν] rather than that God "rested" [ἐπαύσατο]—he asserted a concept of providence as "creatio continua":

130. *Wis.* 9:1.
131. *Wis.* 16:12.
132. Phil. *Opif.* 25 (var.).
133. Phil. *Opif.* 171 (adapted from Yonge).
134. Pl. *Ti.* 30B–C (Jowett).
135. *Wis.* 14:3, 17:2.
136. *Wis.* 12:15, 10:1–12:27.
137. Phil. *Opif.* 11.
138. Phil. *Opif.* 10.

"God never leaves off making, but even as it is the property of fire to burn and of snow to chill, so it is the property of God to make; nay more so by far, inasmuch as He is to all besides the source of action."[139]

By extension, πρόνοια led to παίδευσις.[140] Introducing his exposition of Genesis, Philo insisted on the necessary linkage between cosmogony and the moral order.[141] He praised Moses for having provided here a "cosmogony" [κοσμοποιία] in which "the cosmos is in harmony with the Law, and the Law with the cosmos," and in which man was a true "citizen of the cosmos" [κοσμοπολίτης], indeed, as Wisdom called him, "the father of the cosmos."[142] Philo contrasted this with other codes of law, and by implication other cosmogonies, in which such a linkage was absent. That contrast and criticism seems not to include Timaeus, with its close consideration of "how much attention [the law] has devoted from the very beginning to the Cosmic Order."[143] As a "citizen of the cosmos," and the only one, the first man had received a "divine law" and the "goal of being fully conformed to God."[144] So close was this tie between cosmogony and morality in the providence of God that in the history of the Exodus, the cosmos itself had gone to war in defense of the righteous; so overwhelming was the concept of "virtue" [ἀρετή] that it made even the bane of childlessness tolerable.[145] The statement in Genesis that "God breathed upon his face the breath of life" meant that it was "His will to make compliance with positive ordinances part of duty," lest someone "without experience of virtue" refuse to accept accountability for sin.[146] But when it came to specifying the content of this "virtue," which had certainly been spelled out in the Decalogue of Moses (on which Philo even wrote a separate commentary), the quartet "of divine goods" and virtues formulated by Plato but taught by Sophia came immediately to hand, even in a work supposedly written by King Solomon: "temperance and prudence, justice and fortitude, these are her teaching" [σωφροσύνην γὰρ καὶ φρόνησιν ἐκδιδάσκει, δικαιοσύνην καὶ ἀνδρείαν].[147] Because all creatures

---

139. Phil. Leg. all. 1.5–6; Gn. 2:3.
140. Koch 1932.
141. Phil. Opif. 2–3.
142. Wis. 10:1.
143. Pl. Ti. 24B–C.
144. Phil. Opif. 143–44.
145. Wis. 16:17, 4:1.
146. Gn. 2:7; Phil. Leg. all. 1.35.
147. Wis. 8:7; Pl. Leg. 1.631C. See the discussion of Philo on the Decalogue in Amir 1983, 131–63.

"and man above all" sought after pleasure, the life of virtue had to be one of "self-control" [ἐγκράτεια].[148]

The moral admonition and promise of immortality by the Demiurge to the lesser gods in *Timaeus* bore some parallels to the moral admonition and promise of immortality by God to Adam in *Genesis*. But it has been pointed out by David Winston

> that for Plato, the majority of souls are eventually purified through a process of purgation and thus have a natural claim to immortality, and that the Platonists usually offer proofs for immortality from the very nature of the soul, whereas the author of Wisdom places the emphasis not on this natural claim but on whether one has lived righteously. In so doing, however, he follows the same path pursued by Philo, who implies that only the souls of the wise enjoy immortality. . . . Both he and Philo were undoubtedly influenced in this by biblical tradition.[149]

So in this instance *Genesis* prevailed over *Timaeus*. The "tree of life" in *Genesis,* therefore, represented to Philo "reverence toward God [θεοσέ-βεια], the greatest of the virtues, by means of which the soul attains to immortality [ἀθανατίζεται ἡ ψύχη]," being endowed with an immortality that it had not possessed before by nature.[150] It was of such a life that he spoke in the closing words of *De opificio mundi*, "a life of bliss and blessedness, because he has a character moulded by the truths that piety and holiness enforce."[151] And elsewhere he described being "raised to immortality by virtues."[152] The wicked were dead long before they were buried; "the decent and worthy man, however, does not die by death, but after living long, passes away to eternity, that is, he is borne to eternal life."[153]

But it was especially *Wisdom* that articulated this inseparable connection between immortality and virtue, in a kind of leitmotiv.[154] "God did not make death," it insisted already in its first chapter.[155] On the contrary,

---

148. Phil. *Opif.* 162, 164.
149. Winston 1992, 123.
150. Phil. *Opif.* 154.
151. Phil. *Opif.* 172.
152. Phil. *Conf.* 149.
153. Phil. *Quaes. Gen.* 1.16.
154. Bückers 1938, 10–47; Reese 1970, 62–71.
155. *Wis.* 1:13–14.

it continued, "justice is immortal" [δικαιοσύνη γὰρ ἀθάνατός ἐστιν][156]—
a statement that at least seemed to suggest that immortality was not
natural. "God created man for immortality," it explained, "and made him
the image of his own eternal self; it was the devil's spite that brought death
into the world, and the experience of it is reserved for those who take his
side."[157] Beginning with the consoling assurance that "the souls of the
just are in God's hand," the author granted that "in the eyes of the foolish
they seemed to be dead; their departure was reckoned as defeat"; but in
fact "they have a sure hope of immortality."[158] Immortality and virtue
were inseparable, because "virtue held in remembrance is a kind of immortality."[159] Because of their virtue, therefore, "the just live for
ever."[160] "There is immortality," *Wisdom* defined, "in kinship with wisdom."[161] Then, as if to summarize the inseparability of virtue and immortality and the implicit polemic against the notion of natural immortality, a
later chapter declared, "To know you is the whole of righteousness, and to
acknowledge your power is the root of immortality."[162]

---

156. *Wis.* 1:15.
157. *Wis.* 2:23–24.
158. *Wis.* 3:1–4.
159. *Wis.* 4:1.
160. *Wis.* 5:15.
161. *Wis.* 8:17.
162. *Wis.* 15:3.

V

New Rome: Christ as "God Made Perceptible to the Senses," "Only-Begotten God," and "Image of the God Apprehensible Only to the Mind" (*Timaeus* 92C)

Alexandria would go on being a venue for the confrontation between Athens and Jerusalem and the counterpoint between *Timaeus* and *Genesis*. But the principal locus of the counterpoint now moved from the Alexandrian synagogue to the church of those Middle Platonists and Neoplatonists whom a classic monograph of the nineteenth century called "the Christian Platonists of Alexandria,"[1] including, in the ante-Nicene period, Clement and Origen and, in the Nicene and post-Nicene period, Athanasius and Cyril. On account of its relation to the Alexandrian tradition and specifically to Philo, as well as on account of its doctrine of creation, an especially important case study for the counterpoint is the *Epistle to the Hebrews,* which after considerable hesitation, above all in Rome, was incorporated into the canon of the New Testament.[2] For, on the one hand, summarizing the teaching of *Genesis* and declaring the doctrine of "creatio ex nihilo," it simultaneously invoked and contravened the vocabulary of *Timaeus*[3] when it affirmed that "by faith we perceive [πίστει νοοῦμεν] that the universe was fashioned by the word of God, so that the visible came forth from the invisible";[4] thus it combined a reference to the noun πίστις as Belief (which was for *Timaeus* incompatible with ἀλήθεια) with a reference to the verb derived from νοῦς (which *Timaeus* had made the instrument for perceiving the ἀλήθεια of really real Being, in opposition to δόξα as Belief). On the other hand, that same

---

1. Bigg 1886.
2. Williamson 1970; Dey 1975, 13–20.
3. Pl. *Ti.* 29C–D.
4. *Heb.* 11:3.

chapter of *Hebrews* was also the only place in all of Greek Christian Scripture, whether Septuagint or New Testament, that explicitly called the God of the Bible δημιουργός, indeed τεχνίτης καὶ δημιουργὸς ὁ θεός;[5] this implied a sufficient measure of continuity between *Genesis* and *Timaeus* to warrant use of such well-known technical terms from the vocabulary of the latter to state the teaching of the former on the doctrine of creation.

In addition to Alexandria, each of our other capitals—Jerusalem, Rome, and Athens—retained a privileged position in the Christian thought of the fourth century. Jerusalem, which Irenaeus had already called "the capital city [μητρόπολις] of the citizens of the new covenant,"[6] still occupied a unique place in Christian loyalties, also because of the growing interest in pilgrimage to the Holy Places manifested, for example, by the empress Helena.[7] Likewise, the primacy of Rome as the see of Peter was acknowledged also by Athanasius, bishop of Alexandria, who, having been in 341 the beneficiary of the hospitality of Old Rome while in exile, quoted with approval a letter of the bishop of Rome, Julius I, which insisted that in disputes among churches "the custom has been for word to be written first to us, and then for a just decision to be passed from this place," because that was the prerogative that Rome had "received from the blessed Apostle Peter."[8] Athens, too, would continue to exercise a hold on the mind and the imagination of Christian theologians, one of whom exclaimed as he remembered his student days: "For those who have been comrades there, nothing is so painful as separation from Athens and from one another!"[9]

But that same Christian theologian reserved his grandest rhetorical encomia for another "mighty Christ-loving city," Constantinople as New Rome (of which he would briefly be bishop in 381):

> If it be no great thing to have established and strengthened with wholesome doctrines a city which is the eye of the universe, in its exceeding strength by sea and land, which is, as it were, the link between the Eastern and the Western shores, in which the extremities of the world from every side meet together, and from which, as the common market of the faith, they take their rise, a city borne

5. *Heb.* 11:10. The word δημιουργός is also used in the LXX at 2 *Mc.* 4:1, but with reference to a human being.

6. Iren. *Haer.* 3.12.5.

7. Gr. Nyss. *Ep.* 2; Gr. Naz. *Or.* 42.26.

8. Ath. *Apol. sec.* 2.

9. Gr. Naz. *Or.* 43.24.

hither and thither on the edifying currents of so many tongues, it will be a long time before anything is considered great or worthy of esteem.[10]

For when the emperor Constantine moved the capital of the empire from the banks of the Tiber to the shores of the Bosporus, he set it apart from its classical and pagan predecessor, as the early Byzantine historian Sozomen put it, by seeing to it that "it was not polluted by altars, Grecian temples, or sacrifices."[11] Moreover, as another early Byzantine historian, Socrates Scholasticus, reported, Constantine, "having rendered it equal to imperial Rome, named it 'Constantinople,' establishing by law that it should be designated 'New Rome.'"[12] And it was so designated in the decree of the Second Ecumenical Council, held at Constantinople in 381—"because it is new Rome" [διὰ τὸ εἶναι αὐτὴν νέαν Ῥώμην][13]—and then in the controversial twenty-eighth canon of the Council of Chalcedon in 451, which decreed, "concerning the prerogatives of the most holy church of Constantinople, new Rome" [περὶ τῶν πρεσβείων τῆς ἁγιωτάτης ἐκκλησίας τῆς αὐτῆς Κωνσταντινουπόλεως νέας Ῥώμης], that "the city which is honoured by the imperial power and senate and enjoying privileges equalling older imperial Rome, should also be elevated to her level in ecclesiastical affairs and take second place after her."[14]

In the event, however, Constantinople was not only New Rome; it became a new Athens as well, where the greatest of churches was dedicated not to Saint Peter or even to Saint Andrew, legendary apostle to Byzantium, but to Holy Wisdom, Hagia Sophia, and where Greek wisdom and biblical revelation interacted to produce a full-blown Christian humanism. Within the Christian culture of New Rome, the thought of Clement, Origen, and Athanasius, the three Alexandrian Christian theologians, now went on to be synthesized by the three Cappadocian theologians, Gregory of Nazianzus, Basil of Caesarea, and Gregory of Nyssa, together with Macrina, sister of the latter two; Basil was the author of an important and influential defense of the continued use of classical literature and philosophy by Christians.[15] They continued the counterpoint in the doctrine of creation between the *Timaeus* of Plato and the *Genesis* of

10. Gr. Naz. *Or.* 42.27, 10.
11. Soz. *H.e.* 2.3.
12. Socr. *H.e.* 1.16.
13. Tanner-Alberigo 1:32.
14. Tanner-Alberigo 1:100; see Martin 1951.
15. Pelikan 1993, 10–11.

Moses as it had been developed in Jewish Alexandria.[16] But the doctrines of the incarnation and the Trinity in the Christian orthodoxy that came out of the council held in 325 at Nicaea, and behind those doctrines the language of the Greek New Testament and of the Greek church fathers, made it possible in fourth-century New Rome to connect *Timaeus* and *Genesis* in new ways, as the development of Christian doctrine provided the Cappadocians with a more profound justification for finding such a connection in the closing words of *Timaeus* (translated as these Christian Neoplatonists understood them): "image of the [God who is] apprehensible only to the mind; God made perceptible to the senses; most great and most good, most beautiful and most perfect in His generation—even this one only-begotten Heaven" [εἰκὼν τοῦ νοητοῦ θεὸς αἰσθητός, μέγιστος καὶ ἄριστος κάλλιστός τε καὶ τελεώτατος γέγονεν εἰς οὐρανὸς ὅδε μονογενὴς ὤν].[17] Beginning with the New Testament, many of these Greek vocables had become technical theological terms, applied to Christ as the Logos who had created the world and who became incarnate in Jesus of Nazareth. Thus it was possible for the thought of New Rome to equate the σοφία of Greek wisdom with the σοφία of the *Book of Proverbs* and the *Book of Wisdom,* both of these being attributed to Solomon—not by a collapse of either into the other, but by what we have been calling counterpoint. Or, as Endre von Ivánka has put it, "the Cappadocians remain fully Platonists," but in a way that "the threat to the specifically Christian that lay in these tendencies was overcome, at least in its fundamental essence."[18]

ποιητὴς καὶ πατήρ as the Father of the Lord Jesus Christ[19]

The equating of the God of Moses with Plato's ὁ ὤν was by now an assumption that it was not necessary to substantiate, that it was indeed not possible to controvert; for it was emblazoned in the most "towering text"[20] of the entire Septuagint: the self-designation of the God who spoke to Moses from the burning bush in the words !Εγώ εἰμι ὁ ὤν.[21] The equating may even have been at work in the "intentional *tour de force*" of the salutation of the *Book of Revelation,* ἀπὸ ὁ ὢν καὶ ὁ ἦν καὶ ὁ ἐρχό-

---

16. See Gronau 1914, 36–37.
17. Pl. *Ti.* 92C (adapted from Jowett).
18. Ivánka 1948, 58, 43; see also Callahan 1958.
19. Pl. *Ti.* 28C; *1 Cor.* 8:6; May 1994, 122 n. 19.
20. Murray 1964, 5.
21. *Ex.* 3:14.

μενος, where this version of the divine name remained undeclined despite its being the object of a preposition, as a symbol of its transcendence.[22] But in New Rome the equation acquired new significance and a whole new vocabulary, together with an entire new set of problems, as a consequence of the debates over the Trinity in the fourth century. The eventual outcome of those debates was the adoption of οὐσία (Being), the abstract noun of Greek metaphysics employed by *Timaeus* and derived from the verb εἶναι (to be), to serve as the orthodox and technical term for the Divine as this was shared by Father, Son, and Holy Spirit.[23] But that seemed to run directly contrary to the usage of *Timaeus*, according to which Being (οὐσία) itself was the proper object only of Truth (ἀλήθεια), with Belief (πίστις) being restricted to the questions of Becoming (γένεσις).[24] For now there was a formally legislated and imperially sanctioned πίστις, or creed, "the πίστις [or ἔκθεσις] of the 318 fathers of the Council of Nicaea," the Creed of Nicaea.[25] Contrary to the distinction of *Timaeus*, however, this πίστις had as its object not only the process of Becoming, γένεσις through the divine act of creation, but the divine οὐσία itself, in which the Son of God was said to share because he was, in the celebrated formula of Nicaea proposed by Constantine, apparently at the instance of Bishop Ossius of Cordova, ὁμοούσιος τῷ πατρί.[26] At the same time, that divine οὐσία was identified by the opening words of the Creed of Nicaea: "We believe in one God the Father all powerful, maker of all things both seen and unseen" [Πιστεύομεν εἰς ἕνα θεὸν πατέρα παντοκράτορα, πάντων ὁρατῶν τε καὶ ἀοράτων ποιητήν]. Both the term *one* and the term *God* in this formula referred, according to the theologians of New Rome, to the entire Trinity.[27] This one God was Father all powerful and Maker, and he was therefore, in the words applied by *Timaeus* to the considerably less than all powerful Demiurge, ὁ ποιητής καὶ πατήρ.[28] In the original Creed of Nicaea, the relation of this concept of οὐσία to the concept of ὑπόστασις had been left unclear, as the virtual interchangeability of the two words in the phrase of the creed ἐξ ἑτέρας ὑποστάσεως ἢ οὐσίας made evident. Only in the theological generation of the three Cappadocians did the standard orthodox formula become one

---

22. *Rv.* 1:4; Moulton 1957, 9 n. 1.
23. Prestige 1956, 190–96.
24. Pl. *Ti.* 29C–D.
25. Lampe 1087.
26. Tanner-Alberigo 1:5.
27. Gr. Nyss. *Ref.* 20–21.
28. Pl. *Ti.* 28C.

οὐσία for the Godhead and three ὑποστάσεις for Father, Son, and Holy Spirit. In making their case for the doctrine of the Trinity and its relation to the doctrine of creation, they cited, and applied to the Christian doctrine of the Holy Spirit as the third ὑπόστασις of the Trinity, the words of *Genesis* that "the Spirit of God was being borne up on [ἐπεφέρετο] the face of the water."[29] But they also cited certain "more theologically minded" philosophical writers among the Greeks who had given witness to the doctrine of the Holy Spirit when they "addressed Him as the Mind of the World, or the External Mind, and the like."[30] This seems to be a reference primarily to *Timaeus,* with its doctrine of the world soul, as well as to other Platonic dialogues, such as *Phaedo.*[31] At the same time, however, it was essential to note that the Christian doctrine of the Holy Spirit, in the context of the dogma of the Trinity, differed fundamentally from all such formulations, with their potentially pantheistic implications, by its emphasis on the transcendence of the Spirit and of the Trinity over all the creation in whole or in part.[32]

The Nicene doctrine provided the opportunity for another counterpoint between *Timaeus* and *Genesis,* by supplying further elaboration from *Genesis* for the fundamental thesis of *Timaeus* that "if so be that this Cosmos is beautiful and its Constuctor good, it is plain that he fixed his gaze on the Eternal" [εἰ μὲν δὴ καλός ἐστιν ὅδε ὁ κόσμος ὅ τε δημιουργὸς ἀγαθός, δῆλον ὡς πρὸς τὸ ἀίδιον ἔβλεπεν], because "for Him who is most good [τῷ ἀρίστῳ] it neither was nor is permissible to perform any action save what is most beautiful [τὸ κάλλιστον]."[33] For when the Septuagint *Genesis* reiterated and amplified the refrain "And God saw that it was beautiful" [καὶ εἶδεν ὁ θεὸς ὅτι καλόν],[34] invoking the adjective καλόν, the same word that *Timaeus* had employed to speak about the created world, this, to the theologians of New Rome, required the Trinitarian explanation for both of the key adjectives in that thesis of *Timaeus,* that "whatever is καλόν and whatever is ἀγαθόν, coming from God as it does through the Son, is completed by the instrumentality of the Spirit."[35] This quality of being καλόν, moreover, having been repeated in the *Genesis* cosmogony for each successive order of creatures, was not only an attribute of the

---

29. Bas. *Spir.* 2.6; *Gn.* 1:2; Tarabochia Canavero 1981, 25–28, 37–39.
30. Gr. Naz. *Or.* 31.5.
31. Pl. *Ti.* 35B–37C; Pl. *Phd.* 97C–D.
32. Bas. *Spir.* 22.53.
33. Pl. *Ti.* 29A, 30A (modified from Bury).
34. *Gn.* 1:4, 8, 10, 12, 18, 21, 25, 31.
35. Gr. Nyss. *Maced.*

universe as a whole; "each creature is beautiful in its own way, because in its own way it finds its fulfillment in the Beautiful" [ἐφ’ ἑαυτοῦ ἕκαστον καλόν ἐστι λίαν, ἐφ’ ἑαυτοῦ γὰρ κατὰ τὸν ἴδιον λόγον ἐν τῷ καλῷ συμπεπλή-ρωται].36 But the divine definition of what was καλόν was not the same as the human definition; for "what He esteems beautiful is that which presents in its perfection all the fitness of art, and that which tends to the usefulness of its end." God the Creator was, as he had been portrayed explicitly in *Timaeus* but only implicitly in *Genesis*, "the Supreme Artist, praising each one of His works" in turn and all together.37 For in the plan of the Creator "It is the purpose of the δημιουργία that makes it τὸ καλόν."38

The self-identification of God to Moses as ὁ ὤν, which meant to Philo that only God was true being and that no creatures were,39 meant to the Christian theologians of New Rome, too, that God was not only "the First Nature, but the Only Nature."40 But in their thought it was further re-fined, and fundamentally limited, by the detailed attention they gave to the issues of negative theology, specifically on the Trinitarian grounds that Father, Son, and Holy Spirit were all "unapproachable in thought,"41 and that therefore their relation "ought to have the tribute of our reverent silence."42 In that apophatic enterprise they were aided by their interpretations both of *Genesis* and of *Timaeus*. A key text of *Timaeus*, as has been noted earlier, was the admission that "To discover the Maker and Father of this Universe were a task indeed; and having discovered Him, to declare Him unto all men were a thing impossible" [τὸν μὲν οὖν ποιητὴν καὶ πατέρα τοῦδε τοῦ παντὸς εὑρεῖν τε ἔργον καὶ εὑρόντα εἰς πάντας ἀδύνατον λέγειν].43 Origen spent a substantial portion of his response to the Hellenistic philosopher Celsus on this "noble and impressive" text. "But consider," he argued, "whether there is not more regard for the needs of mankind when the divine word introduces the divine Logos, who was in the beginning with God, as becoming flesh, that the Logos, of whom Plato says that after finding him it is impossible to declare him to all men, might be able to reach anybody." Conceding that "we certainly maintain

36. Gr. Nyss. *Hex.*
37. Bas. *Hex.* 3.10.
38. Bas. *Hex.* 4.6.
39. Phil. *V. Mos.* 1.75.
40. Gr. Naz. *Or.* 28.31.
41. Bas. *Spir.* 22.53.
42. Gr. Naz. *Or.* 29.8.
43. Pl. *Ti.* 28C.

that it is difficult to see the Maker and Father of the universe," Origen insisted that "anyone who has understood how we must think of the only-begotten God, the Son of God, the firstborn of all creation, and how that the Logos became flesh, will see that anyone will come to know the Father and Maker of this universe by looking at the image of the invisible God."[44]

Gregory Nazianzus, citing this text from *Timaeus* without identifying its specific source, paraphrased it to mean that Plato was "subtly suggesting, I think, by the word 'difficult' his own apprehension, yet avoiding our test of it by claiming it was impossible to describe."[45] Invoking the concept of "the knowledge of the divine Essence" [τῆς θείας οὐσίας τὴν γνῶσιν], Gregory of Nyssa, in his *Life of Moses*—Moses being "by far the best-known figure of Jewish history in the pagan world"[46] and the one man who above all could have claimed direct knowledge of the divine οὐσία after confronting it on Mount Sinai, where God had spoken to him, Basil said, "in person and without enigmas"[47]—unequivocally asserted that, not only for human beings including Moses but even for angels, God was "to be distinguished only by means of negation" [τῇ ἀποφάσει ταύτῃ διοριζόμενος].[48] But in placing its far-reaching apophatic limitation on all language about the Divine, *Timaeus* had added a stipulation, which, in the context of the dialogue, may have seemed harmless enough, but which, at the hands of Hellenistic Jewish thought in Alexandria and then especially at the hands of Christian thought in New Rome, provided grounds for reinterpreting *Timaeus* in the light of *Genesis,* a *Genesis* that was itself being reinterpreted now in the light of the New Testament. The distinction of *Timaeus* between "the Truth" [τὸ ἀληθές] and "the likely account" [τὸ εἰκός], according to which both *Genesis* and *Timaeus* had to be seen as only "likely accounts" because they dealt with Becoming rather than with Being, had added the remote hypothetical possibility that "only if God concurred [θεοῦ ξυμφήσαντος] could we dare to affirm that our account is true."[49] But now Christianity in New Rome was claiming to the Greeks, as Judaism in Alexandria already had, that God truly had "concurred," and mightily, through acts of divine intervention and words of divine revelation. From this it followed that this account of Becoming as re-

---

44. Or. *Cels.* 7.42–43. See the comments of Andresen 1955, 132–35, 347–50.
45. Gr. Naz. *Or.* 28.4.
46. Gager 1972, 18; see also Jean Rousselet in Vignaux 1973, 95–113.
47. Bas. *Hex.* 6.1; see Früchtel 1968, 110–12.
48. Gr. Nyss. *V. Mos.* 2.
49. Pl. *Ti.* 72D.

corded in *Genesis* could claim to be not only "a likely account" but a "true" one.

One of the most pervasive of the definitional presuppositions in *Timaeus* was the statement that the act of creation had taken place when the Demiurge "brought [the cosmos] into order out of disorder" [εἰς τάξιν . . . ἐκ τῆς ἀταξίας].[50] Arguing against what, fairly or unfairly, he took to be the effort of the heretic Eunomius to put the two sources of knowledge, "nature itself and the divine laws," on the same level, Gregory of Nyssa maintained that for the question of "the divine generation," the relation of the Son to the Father from eternity, nature was "not trustworthy for instruction." This would apply, he continued, "even if one were to take the universe itself as an illustration of the argument." For by contrast with the eternal and timeless generation of the Son by the Father, there "also ran through the creation [of the universe] the measure of time, meted out in a certain order and arrangement by stated days and nights, for each of the things that came into being." As his authority for this view of the universe and of time, he cited what "we learn in the cosmogony of Moses."[51] The process described in that cosmogony was the creation through the Word in *Genesis* as an "ordering of the world into a cosmos" [διακόσμησις], a term that appeared in Plato's *Timaeus* in the form of a participle used substantively about the creator gods as οἱ διακοσμοῦντες and then as a noun for the process in Aristotle's *Metaphysics*; verb or noun, it suited well what *Genesis* taught, which was why Philo had also employed it.[52]

The Incarnate Logos as "God Made Perceptible to the Senses" [θεὸς αἰσθητός][53]

As an intensification of this apophatic limitation on language about divine Being, *Timaeus* had declared, in yet another such stipulation, "The principles which are still higher than these are known only to God and to the man who is dear to God" [τὰς δ' ἔτι τούτων ἀρχὰς ἄνωθεν θεὸς οἶδε καὶ ἀνδρῶν ὅς ἂν ἐκείνῳ φίλος ᾖ].[54] Whatever Plato may have meant by this added possibility, Moses seemed to be a highly likely candidate for this position of "the man who is dear to God," and it was as such that Philo

---

50. Pl. *Ti.* 30A.
51. Gr. Nyss. *Eun.* 3.7.34.
52. Pl. *Ti.* 75D; Arist. *Met.* A.986a6; Gr. Nyss. *Or. dom.* 2; Phil. *Opif.* 20.
53. Pl. *Ti.* 92C; *Jn.* 1:14.
54. Pl. *Ti.* 53D.

had identified him, as one who was eligible to discover by divine revelation those very "principles which are still higher than these [and which] are known only to God and to the man who is dear to God." Philo's *Life of Moses* was a detailed biographical and theological account of "this greatest and most perfect of men."[55] But when Gregory of Nyssa undertook to write his own *Life of Moses* several centuries later, he was able to identify a new prime candidate for the position: if "the principles which are still higher than these are known only to God and to the man who is dear to God," then Jesus Christ was, by orthodox teaching, both "God" in the fullest and strictest sense and at the same time in a unique sense "the man who is dear to God," and he was therefore the only one who was qualified on both counts to know and to reveal "the principles which are still higher than these." He who was, in the words of the *Gospel of John*, the Logos made incarnate was, in the words of *Timaeus,* "God made perceptible to the senses" [θεὸς αἰσθητός].[56]

To make this point, the Greek-speaking Christian theologians of New Rome unabashedly took over, as "the scriptural conception of an intelligible world," the distinction of *Timaeus* between the world perceptible to the senses, κόσμος αἰσθητός, which was subject to Becoming, and the world apprehensible only to the mind, κόσμος νοητός, which alone could be said to have really real Being.[57] Thus in his commentary on the cosmogony of *Genesis,* Basil of Caesarea taught a double creation: first of "this invisible world," populated by various nonphysical existences, including angels; and then of "a new world, both a school and a training place where the souls of men should be taught and a home for beings destined to be born and to die," the world of "animals and plants," and, most important of all, a world dominated by "the succession of time, forever pressing on and passing away and never stopping in its course."[58] Similarly, Gregory of Nyssa postulated the distinction between, on the one hand, what was αἰσθητὸν καὶ ὑλῶδες and, on the other hand, what was νοητόν τε καὶ ἄϋλον.[59] He could go so far as to declare that "the ultimate division of all being is into τὸ νοητόν and τὸ αἰσθητόν."[60] As their authority for putting in place all of this conceptual apparatus from *Timaeus,* both Basil and Gregory cited "the apostle," namely, Paul, who had

55. Phil. *V. Mos.* 1.1.
56. *Jn.* 1:14; Pl. *Ti.* 92C.
57. Wolfson 1956, 268–69; Pl. *Ti.* 29C.
58. Bas. *Hex.* 1.5.
59. Gr. Nyss. *Cant.* 6.
60. Gr. Nyss. *Eun.* 1.270–71.

"broadly" referred to τὸ αἰσθητόν as τὰ ὁρατά and to τὸ νοητόν as τὰ ἀόρατα.[61] On the basis of measurable differences in quantity, quality, and other empirically perceptible characteristics, it was possible to compare and classify whatever belonged to the κόσμος αἰσθητός; but there was no place for such differentiation within the κόσμος νοητός, where the basis for making distinctions was the degree of free will, that is, participation in the First Good.[62]

Gregory of Nazianzus, too, made use of this distinction from *Timaeus* to divide the process of creation described in the cosmogony of *Genesis* as consisting of two stages, corresponding to the κόσμος νοητός as "His first creation," which was a "nature akin to Deity," and the κόσμος αἰσθητός as "a second world, material and visible," which was a nature "utterly alien to [Deity]"; and he went on to a glowing description of the resulting inner "harmony and union of the whole" that prevailed in the perceptible world as a system.[63] Elsewhere he defined it as the superiority of those angelic existences which participated in τὸ νοητόν that they could "mingle with one another as well as with bodies, incorporeally and invisibly," and could thus comprehend the entire "system of things, visible and invisible."[64] Belonging as they did to the same order of reality as God, by virtue of their being beyond the reach of the senses, these existences were "far higher in nature and nearer to God than we."[65] If it was accurate, in the phraseology of Gregory of Nyssa, to speak of this dichotomy of *Timaeus* between κόσμος νοητός and κόσμος αἰσθητός as "the ultimate division of all being,"[66] then the concluding particularization of it by *Timaeus* in the phrase θεὸς αἰσθητός[67] would seem ideally suited to the Christian purpose of finding in the incarnate Logos the fulfillment of the Timaean divine principle of creative mediation.

But here there was a tension between *Timaeus* and *Genesis*, at any rate as *Genesis* and *Timaeus* were being read in Christian New Rome, and it probably took the heretical challenges of the fourth century to make that tension evident. In its celebratory paraphrase of the cosmogony of *Genesis*, the eighth chapter of the *Book of Proverbs* had represented personified Wisdom, Sophia, as saying of herself, "The Lord *created* me as

61. Col. 1:16.
62. Gr. Nyss. *Eun.* 1.272–74; Bas. *Hex.* 1.5.
63. Gr. Naz. *Or.* 38.10.
64. Gr. Naz. *Ep.* 101.
65. Gr. Naz. *Or.* 28.3.
66. Gr. Nyss. *Eun.* 1.270–71.
67. Pl. *Ti.* 92C.

the beginning [or root principle] of his ways for his works" [κύριος ἔκτισέν με ἀρχὴν ὁδῶν αὐτοῦ εἰς ἔργα αὐτοῦ], employing here the technical term meaning "create," κτίζειν, rather than the less specific term used in the first verse of the Septuagint and meaning "make," ποιεῖν.[68] In his *Orations against the Arians* Athanasius had labored over that verse from *Proverbs* at greater length than over any other passage of Scripture, resorting to everything from textual criticism to analogy to the authority of the creed in order to prove that this did not make the eternal Son of God a creature.[69] A similar danger to Nicene orthodoxy lurked in calling the dichotomy between κόσμος νοητός and κόσμος αἰσθητός in *Timaeus* "the ultimate division of all being." Immediately after saying that, therefore, Gregory of Nyssa added: "Reason again divides this 'which is not seen' into the uncreated and the created."[70] So also Gregory of Nazianzus, immediately after characterizing the angelic "nature" [φύσις] in the κόσμος νοητός as "far higher and nearer to God than we," hastened to specify that it was nevertheless "farther distant from God, and from the complete comprehension of his nature [φύσις], than it is lifted above our complex and lowly and earthward-sinking composition."[71] Against superstition and idolatry it may have been acceptable for the Judaism of Alexandria, and then for the Christianity of Alexandria and New Rome, to appropriate the separation of *Timaeus* between τὸ νοητόν and τὸ αἰσθητόν and to locate the God of *Genesis* within the first of those categories. But the doctrine of the incarnation located the Son of God in both categories, and the heretical version of that doctrine made it obligatory to find Nyssen's "ultimate division of all being"[72] where *Genesis* had unambiguously drawn the line—as Gregory put it later on in the same treatise, in a "conception of existences divided into two, the creation and the uncreated Nature,"[73] the division into creature and Creator—and to put the divine Logos on the Creator's side of that boundary and the human nature assumed by the Logos on the other side. "We believe in one God the Father all powerful, maker of all things both seen and unseen" [Πιστεύομεν εἰς ἕνα θεὸν πατέρα παντοκράτορα, πάντων ὁρατῶν τε καὶ ἀοράτων ποιητήν]—by these opening words, which repeated the Shema, the Niceno-Constantinopolitan Creed, adopted at New Rome in 381, still

---

68. *Prv.* 8:22; *Gn.* 1:1. See Bauer 455–56, 680–81; Lampe 782–83, 1107.
69. Ath. *Ar.* 2.16.18–2.22.82.
70. Gr. Nyss. *Eun.* 1.270–71.
71. Gr. Naz. *Or.* 28.3.
72. Gr. Nyss. *Eun.* 1.270–71.
73. Gr. Nyss. *Eun.* 3.3.2.

shared with *Timaeus* the distinction between the visible realm and the invisible realm, but it affirmed with *Genesis* that the one God was the transcendent Creator of both realms rather than a component of the invisible realm. "For wide and insurmountable is the interval that divides and fences off uncreated from created nature" [πολὺ γὰρ τὸ μέσον καὶ ἀδιεξίτητον, ᾧ πρὸς τὴν κτιστὴν οὐσίαν ἡ ἄκτιστος φύσις διατετείχισται].[74] Once the Timaean vocabulary was "fenced off" this way, the orthodox doctrine of the incarnation could make good use of it.

The Son as "the Only-Begotten God [ὁ μονογενὴς θεός]"[75]

By retaining the dichotomy of *Timaeus* between that which was apprehensible only to the mind, τὸ νοητόν, and that which was perceptible to the senses, τὸ αἰσθητόν, and by subordinating it to the most fundamental dichotomy of all, that of *Genesis* between the created and the Uncreated, the Christian orthodoxy of New Rome was compelled to consider the ultimate implications of many other terms and concepts that were shared by the two traditions. That obligation applied with special force to those items of common property that were now being applied to Christ as Son of God, among which none carried more far-reaching Christological and Trinitarian connotations than the Timaean, and now Johannine, epithet μονογενής.

The last two words of *Timaeus,* μονογενὴς ὤν,[76] in which R. D. Archer-Hind found "virtually summed up Plato's whole system of idealistic monism,"[77] also summed up the earlier and more ample statement "Its Maker made neither two Universes nor an infinite number, but there is and will continue to be this one generated Heaven, unique of its kind [εἷς ὅδε μονογενὴς οὐρανὸς γεγονὼς ἔστι τε καὶ ἔτ' ἔσται]."[78] Μονογενές was one of the twenty-one epithets attributed to Sophia in the *Book of Wisdom.*[79] From one or another source, including perhaps one or both of these, the term μονογενής became part of the technical vocabulary of the *Gospel of John* for the Son of God, appearing there four times in all, all four of them in its first three chapters.[80] The shift in the English rendering of the word,

---

74. Gr. Nyss. *Eun.* 2.67–69.
75. Pl. *Ti.* 92C; *Jn.* 1:18.
76. Pl. *Ti.* 92C.
77. Archer-Hind 1888, 345 n. 8.
78. Pl. *Ti.* 31B.
79. *Wis.* 7:22.
80. *Jn.* 1:14, 1:18, 3:16, 3:18.

from the earlier "only-begotten" of the Authorized Version (which reflected the consistent use of "unigenitus" by the Vulgate of these passages as well as by the Latin of the Nicene Creed and the "Gloria in excelsis" of the Mass), to the simple "only" favored by twentieth-century versions, is an indication of changes in the scholarly opinion about the term μονογενής itself, as well as of shifts in modern theology. But the most arresting appearance of the word is part of a textual variant in the *Gospel of John:* "No one has ever seen God; but the only-begotten God [μονογενὴς θεός], he who is nearest to the Father's heart, he has made him known."[81] This variant reading is so well attested in the manuscripts that "more and more critical texts have adopted θεός; however, commentators and translators have been generally reluctant to accept that reading as the original or as the better of the two available readings,"[82] for whatever reason. Both parts of the verse figured prominently in the thought of New Rome. The first half was one of the key texts in support of Cappadocian apophaticism, and it was so used, for example, when Gregory of Nyssa quoted it together with other passages to prove that the essence of God was "so inaccessible that our mind can nowhere approach God."[83] But the second half, with its textual variant, was important for Basil of Caesarea and especially his brother Gregory of Nyssa, who throughout his writings referred to the Son of God as ὁ μονογενὴς θεός, a reading to which, interestingly, his Arian opponent Eunomius does not appear to have objected. Another and cognate variant, which went back to earlier patristic Greek writers and which was carried over into the manuscripts of their works, was the confusion between γεννητός (begotten) and γενητός (made).[84]

The two variants had a theological relation, not only an etymological one. The burden of the Cappadocian case against Arian heresy was to argue that as the μονογενής, indeed ὁ μονογενὴς θεός, the Son of God was not to be ranked with creatures, not even as the supreme creature through whom all the "other" creatures had been created, but as Creator. Making that case obliged them to cope with the issue of the relation between the cosmogonies of *Timaeus* and *Genesis;* for the term appeared in *Timaeus,* not in *Genesis,* where it could be discovered only by reading into the text of *Genesis* the miniature cosmogony of the prologue to the *Gospel of*

---

81. *Jn.* 1:18.
82. McReynolds 1981, 105.
83. Gr. Nyss. *Beat.* 6.
84. Lampe 310–11, 312–13.

John, as when, for example, Basil professed to have found in *Genesis* "clear proofs of the μονογενής."[85] The question was whether the identification of the Son of God with the first of the pregnant phrases at the end of *Timaeus* necessitated, or justified, the identification of him also with the last of them: if θεὸς αἰσθητός, defined and circumscribed by a strict monotheism, accurately described the incarnate Son of God, did μονογενὴς ὤν, similarly defined and circumscribed, do so also for the preexistent Son of God?[86]

In a summary answer to that question, which invoked the variant reading ὁ μονογενὴς θεός, Basil of Caesarea insisted that "inasmuch as all created nature, both this visible world and all that is conceived of in the mind, cannot hold together without the care and providence of God," it had to depend not on another creature but on nothing less than "the Creator Logos, the only-begotten God."[87] The answer of Gregory of Nyssa, as developed particularly in book 3 of his *Contra Eunomium,* was more detailed. He attacked the attempt of Eunomius to find a uniqueness for the μονογενής in the general circumstance "that everything which you conceive by itself is incapable of comparison with the universe, and with the individual things which compose it," as though that were an adequate way to make the distinction between Creator and creature.[88] The need for such a distinction also rendered nugatory, in the discussion of "the nature of the only-begotten God," the explanation that "it would not have been had it not been constructed," for "what else is there among the things we contemplate in the creation which exists without being made? Heaven, earth, air, sea—everything whatever that is, surely is by being made."[89] But that applied to creatures, not to the only-begotten God. The distinction had to be clear-cut and ontological: "The μονογενής is something other than the nature of the universe," because of the statement of the *Gospel of John* that "through him all things came to be"; therefore, "since all things are from God, and the Son is God, the creation is properly something other than the Godhead."[90] Because of the distinction, it was to "the μονογενὴς θεός, who created the ages," that the beginning of each individual creature was to be traced: "vegetation, fruits, the generation of

85. Bas. *Hex.* 3.4.
86. Pl. *Ti.* 92C.
87. Bas. *Spir.* 8.19.
88. Gr. Nyss. *Eun.* 3.2.23–24.
89. Gr. Nyss. *Eun.* 3.2.154.
90. Gr. Nyss. *Eun.* 3.5.31, quoting *Jn.* 1:3.

animals, the formation of man, appeared at the time when each of these things seemed expedient to the wisdom of the Creator."[91]

Therefore when the creed of Eunomius attempted to vindicate the sovereignty of God the Creator and, by implication, to reduce the status of the Only-begotten by declaring that God "did not stand in need, in the act of creation, of matter or parts or natural instruments," Gregory of Nyssa agreed and paraphrased the words of Eunomius to mean that "the power and wisdom of God has no need of any external assistance." But that did not apply to the only-begotten God, as though he had been some sort of created "instrument" in the act of creating the cosmos; for he was in fact that very "Power of God and Wisdom of God" in person, which had no need of any external assistance.[92] Rather it was true that the creation of the cosmos itself, as well as subsequently "every operation [ἐνέργεια] that extends from God to creation and is designated according to our differing conceptions of it," was Trinitarian in basic structure, "having its origin in the Father, proceeding through the Son, and reaching its completion by the Holy Spirit" [ἐκ πατρὸς ἀφορμᾶται καὶ διὰ τοῦ υἱοῦ πρόεισι καὶ ἐν τῷ πνεύματι τῷ ἁγίῳ τελειοῦται].[93] Eunomius also claimed that the eternity of the creating Logos would have to imply the eternity of the things that had been created,[94] which was really meant as an argument for the converse proposition, that both the creating Logos and the "other" creatures were temporal rather than eternal. To this the response was, once again, the sharpest possible distinction between the two with regard to time: "The begetting of the Son does not fall within time, any more than the creation was before time, so that it can in no kind of way be right to partition the indivisible, and, by declaring that there was a time when the Author of all existence was not, to insert this false idea of time into the creative Source of the Universe."[95] When Scripture spoke about the "begetting" of the Son and therefore called him μονογενής, it was, by a process of definition through exclusion, utilizing "all the forms of generation that human intelligence recognizes" but filtering out all "the corporeal senses attaching to the words," in order to be able "to set forth the ineffable power of God"[96] and thus to describe the indescribable process of creation through the Word of God.

91. Gr. Nyss. *Eun.* 3.7.5.
92. Gr. Nyss. *Ref.* 68–69, quoting *I Cor.* 1:24.
93. Gr. Nyss. *Tres dii.*
94. Gr. Nyss. *Eun.* 3.6.60.
95. Gr. Nyss. *Eun.* 1.381.
96. Gr. Nyss. *Ref.* 89–94.

"Imago Dei" and Christ as "Image of the God Who Is Apprehensible Only to the Mind [εἰκὼν τοῦ νοητοῦ]"[97]

All of that reasoning had direct implications for the doctrine of man, which was for both *Timaeus* and *Genesis* the climax and goal of their cosmogony.[98] When Basil composed his *Hexaemeron*, he had that goal in mind but did not quite reach it; in the final discourse, he promised, "If God permits, we will say later in what way man was created in the image of God, and how he shares this resemblance," but he never got to it.[99] When, therefore, his brother Gregory of Nyssa undertook his treatise *On the Creation of Man*, he connected it to Basil's commentary on *Genesis*, in which, because of the shortness of time, "the consideration of man was lacking."[100] The counterpoint of the statement at the beginning of *Genesis* that God created man "in our image, after our likeness" [κατ' εἰκόνα ἡμετέραν καὶ καθ' ὁμοίωσιν],[101] with the phrase at the close of *Timaeus* about the "image of [the God who is] apprehensible only to the mind" [εἰκὼν τοῦ νοητοῦ][102] and with its earlier declaration "that the similar is infinitely more beautiful than the dissimilar"[103] had been exploited already by Philo, for whom the "pattern" [παράδειγμα] of the image was the divine Logos, because Adam—and "as far as their mind was concerned" [κατὰ τὴν διάνοιαν], later human beings as well"[104]— "was made an image and copy" [ἀπεικόνισμα καὶ μίμημα] of the Logos.[105] And that which had been created in the image of God "must of necessity be beautiful [καλόν]."[106]

To the Christian theologians of New Rome the orthodox doctrine of the incarnation meant that Jesus Christ could take over not only the title of "God made perceptible to the senses" from *Timaeus* but also this associated and corollary title of "image of [the God who is] apprehensible only to the mind."[107] Thus the concept of the "imago Dei" in both *Genesis* and *Timaeus* acquired a specificity that neither of the two cos-

97. Pl. *Ti.* 92C; *Col.* 1:15.
98. Pl. *Ti.* 90E.
99. Bas. *Hex.* 9.6.
100. Gr. Nyss. *Hom. opif.* ep. ded.
101. *Gn.* 1:26.
102. Pl. *Ti.* 92C.
103. Pl. *Ti.* 33B.
104. Phil. *Opif.* 145–46.
105. Phil. *Opif.* 139.
106. Pl. *Ti.* 28A.
107. Pl. *Ti.* 92C.

mogonies had itself provided, but that a reading of each in the light of the other, and more importantly a reading of both in the light of Christology, could now supply. The biblical proof for this method came from the very phraseology of *Genesis* that had seemed so problematic in the light of biblical monotheism: "Let us make man according to our image and likeness" [Ποιήσωμεν ἄνθρωπον κατ᾽ εἰκόνα ἡμετέραν καὶ καθ᾽ ὁμοί-ωσιν].[108] For, Basil of Caesarea argued, "To whom does he say, 'in our image,' to whom if not to him who is 'the effulgence of his splendor and the stamp of his very being' and 'the image of the invisible God'? It is, then, to his living image, to him who has said 'My Father and I are one' and 'Anyone who has seen me has seen the Father,' that God says 'Let us make man in our image.'"[109] But this identification of the preexistent second ὑπόστασις of the Trinity as both the addressee of the words "Let us make man in our image" and the pattern (παράδειγμα) for the image went beyond the Philonic identification of image and Logos by equating that preexistent Logos with the Incarnate One through whom God had brought about "the restoration of the image" [τὴν τῆς εἰκόνος ἐπανάληψιν].[110]

This restoration was, in one sense, a process of "new modeling us from the evil mould of sin once more to his own image";[111] but, more profoundly, it represented a new "sequence and order" [ἀκολουθία καὶ τάξις] that went beyond mere restoration.[112] The difference between the two was rooted in the incarnation, "inasmuch as then [in the first creation of the image] he imparted the better nature, whereas now [being the Image in person] he himself partakes of the worse" through the incarnation, in order thereby to communicate a second image and "a second communion far more marvelous than the first."[113] Being renewed "according to the image and likeness of the first and the only and the true Beauty" [κατ᾽ εἰκόνα καὶ ὁμοίωσιν τοῦ πρώτου καὶ μόνου καὶ ἀληθινοῦ κάλλους], there-fore, was synonymous with "being conformed to Christ."[114] The inter-weaving of Timaean and biblical motifs in such a statement was of a piece with the Cappadocians' use of the other formulas contained in the close of *Timaeus*. Rationality, freedom, and immortality, the three component

---

108. *Gn.* 1:26.
109. Bas. *Hex.* 9.6, quoting *Heb.* 1:3, *Col.* 1:5, *Jn.* 10:30, and *Jn.* 14:9.
110. Gr. Nyss. *Or. dom.* 2.
111. Gr. Nyss. *Ref.* 112.
112. Gr. Nyss. *Cant.* 15.
113. Gr. Naz. *Or.* 38.13.
114. Gr. Nyss. *Cant.* 15, quoting *Phil.* 3:10.

elements of the image of God in Cappadocian thought,[115] all manifested such an interweaving. But the Christological and the eschatological content of the image enabled them to read each of these three component elements back into the creation account of *Genesis* and thereby also to supplement and correct the creation account of *Timaeus*, since both accounts had spoken of the image of God.[116]

One way this was done with respect to the doctrine of the image of God was to give *Genesis* preference over *Timaeus* in identifying the primary locus of the image. For *Timaeus* described the cosmos as made in the image, while *Genesis* applied it specifically and exclusively to the creation of man; Philo extrapolated that doctrine of the creation of man to the κόσμος αἰσθητός, seen as having been created in the image of the κόσμος νοητός.[117] But despite the attractiveness of the doctrine of the image in *Timaeus*, Gregory of Nyssa declared the image to be the unique quality of the human creature, "not of the heavens nor the moon nor the sun nor the beauty of the stars nor any of the other phenomena of creation."[118] Gregory Nazianzus, too, invoked the complexity of various creatures—animals, fish, birds, insects, plants, sea, sky, stars, and sun—to prove that human understanding could not grasp even the rest of the natural world, much less the essence of the Divine.[119] Therefore when Gregory of Nyssa undertook the composition of his work *On the Creation of Man* as a continuation of his brother's exposition of the cosmogony of *Genesis*, which had gone into great detail about the beauty of the created world, he explicitly declared that the creation of man was "second to none of the wonders of the world, perhaps even greater than any of those known to us, because no other existing thing except the human creation has been made like God."[120] Because of the image, including its quality of rationality, man was unique, despite "having taken up into himself every single form of life, both that of plants and that which is seen in brutes."[121] Like the brutes, the human creature was "subject to flux and change," but "the element of our soul which is in the likeness of God is stable and unalterable [τὸ μόνιμόν τε καὶ ὡσαύτως ἔχον]."[122] Although only God possessed

---

115. Pelikan 1993, 126–34.
116. Gr. Nyss. *Or. catech.* 6.
117. Phil. *Opif.* 24–25.
118. Gr. Nyss. *Cant.* 2.
119. Gr. Naz. *Or.* 28.22–30.
120. Gr. Nyss. *Hom. opif.* ep. ded.
121. Gr. Nyss. *Anim. res.*
122. Gr. Nyss. *Hom. opif.* 27.

true "blessedness" [μακαριότης], it was uniquely possible for man, "because he who fashioned him made him in the image of God," to be called blessed as well, "through participation" [κατὰ μετουσίαν].[123]

At least indirectly traceable to *Timaeus*, and perhaps to intermediate sources, was another aspect of the doctrine of man and the image in Gregory of Nyssa. *Timaeus* had explained the origin of "women and the whole female sex"[124] as a form of punishment: "According to the probable account, all those creatures generated as men who proved themselves cowardly and spent their lives in wrong-doing were transformed, at their second becoming, into women."[125] According to Philo, although "woman, too, was made" [ἐπλάσθη καὶ γύνη] by God the Creator,[126] the human being first created in the image of God had been "neither male nor female."[127] Gregory of Nyssa took advantage of the shift of pronouns from singular to plural in the statement "God made man, according to the image of God he made him [αὐτόν], male and female he made them [αὐτούς]"[128] to introduce a caesura into the middle of that statement: "The creation of our nature is in a sense twofold [διπλῆ], one made like to God, the other divided according to this distinction" of male and female. The first of these creations, that which took place according to the image of God, pertained to "the rational and intelligent element, which does not admit the distinction of male and female"; therefore, despite the masculine singular pronoun "him" [αὐτόν], it was not masculine but neither masculine nor feminine. The second creation was responsible for "our bodily form and structure," divided into male and female. And to make clear that "that which was made 'in the image' is one thing [without gender], and that which is now manifested in wretchedness [with gender] is another," Moses in *Genesis* had, by the inspiration of the Holy Spirit, chosen his words so carefully when he wrote, "And God made man, according to the image of God he made him [αὐτόν], male and female he made them [αὐτούς]."[129]

In making this case for the Nicene declaration that the Son of God was of the same nature with the Father, Basil analyzed the doxology in *Romans* 11:36: "Source, Guide, and Goal of all that is [ἐξ αὐτοῦ καὶ δι' αὐτοῦ

---

123. Gr. Nyss. *Beat.* 1.
124. Pl. *Ti.* 91D.
125. Pl. *Ti.* 90E (modified from Bury).
126. Phil. *Opif.* 151.
127. Phil. *Opif.* 134.
128. *Gn.* 1:27.
129. Gr. Nyss. *Hom. opif.* 16; Armstrong 1948, 120–21.

καὶ εἰς αὐτὸν τὰ πάντα]—to him [αὐτῷ] be glory for ever! Amen." He applied that doxology specifically to the ὑπόστασις of the Son:

> For from him [ἐξ αὐτοῦ], for all things that are, comes the cause of their being, according to the will of God the Father. Through him [δι᾿ αὐτοῦ] all things have their continuance and constitution, for he created all things, and metes out to each severally what is necessary for its health and preservation. Therefore to him [εἰς αὐτόν] all things are turned, looking with irresistible longing and unspeakable affection to "the author" and maintainer "of" their "life."[130]

But thanks to the amplification of the Nicene declaration that Basil and the other two Cappadocians, together with others of their contemporaries, had formulated as the orthodox doctrine of the Trinity at the First Council of Constantinople in 381, which laid down the Niceno-Constantinopolitan Creed, that same passage became the basis for a speculative Trinitarian metaphysic in which not only all of Scripture, including and especially *Genesis,* but all of human thought generally, including and especially *Timaeus,* could find a place. That metaphysic was the achievement above all of Augustine and Boethius in Catholic Rome.

---

130. Bas. *Spir.* 5.7.

VI

Catholic Rome: The Trinity as "Source, Guide, and Goal" (*Timaeus* 27C–42D)

The translation of the Hebrew of *Genesis* into the vocabulary of the Greeks (even, to some considerable degree, into the vocabulary of *Timaeus*) enabled the Jews of Alexandria, then the Christians of Alexandria, and then the Christians of New Rome to read the two texts in a new and contrapuntal way. So in turn the translation of the Greek of *Timaeus* into the vocabulary of the Romans, together with the production of the Latin *Genesis*, enabled the Christian philosophers of Catholic Rome to take up that task after their own special fashion and, in so doing, to distance themselves from the philosophers of classical Rome, including Lucretius, just as Lucretius had distanced himself from the Roman religious tradition.[1] *Timaeus* was among the several works of Greek literature that were translated into Latin, in whole or in part, by Cicero; but of this translation only fragments have survived.[2] The first half of *Timaeus* (17–53C) was translated into Latin again in the fourth century, by Calcidius (or Chalcidius), who was probably a Christian and who also composed a commentary on this portion of the dialogue.[3] The work bears the dedication "Osio suo,"[4] and the manuscript tradition of the work identified the dedicatee as the Catholic bishop of Cordova, Ossius (or Hosius), theological counselor to Constantine and chairman at the Council of Nicaea in 325, where he played a prominent role in the history of the development of the doctrine of the Trinity and is thought to have been the source for its most celebrated formula, the ὁμοούσιος.[5] It is, however, generally sup-

---

1. See Troncarelli 1987, 61–64, on the subsequent role of this Christian use of Plato to refute Lucretius.
2. Giomini 1975, 177–227.
3. See Waszink 1964, 25; 1975, xi–xii.
4. Cal. *Ti.* ep. ded. 3.
5. Cf. Switalski 1902, 1–2.

posed that Augustine read *Timaeus* in the translation of Cicero, not in that of Calcidius.[6]

Catholic Rome, in the person of Jerome, preserved in the Latin translation and paraphrase of the *Chronicles* of Eusebius "the most abundant information we possess about the life of the poet" Lucretius, on which even present-day scholarship is obliged to rely.[7] And it was to another writer of Catholic Rome, the Latin apologist Lactantius, that Lucretius owed a measure of his reputation in the Latin Middle Ages; Lactantius considered Lucretius "his second most favoured Roman poet," right after Vergil, and in some of his quotations from *De rerum natura*, "Lactantius . . . used an earlier state of the tradition" than that of the manuscripts we now possess.[8] In his *Divine Institutes* Lactantius also quoted the locus classicus from "Plato in the *Timaeus*," to the effect that "the energy and majesty" of God were "so great that no one can either conceive it in his mind, or give utterance to it in words, on account of his surpassing and incalculable power" [ut eam neque mente concipere neque uerbis enarrare quisquam possit ob nimiam et inaestimabilem potestatem]; the passage seems to have come to him through Minucius Felix.[9] In a later work, his *Epitome of the Divine Institutes,* he more amply and more accurately quoted these words of Plato "on the worship of the God whom he acknowledged to be the Maker and Father of things [conditorem rerum et parentem]," together with the following passage that God "is good and, being jealous of no one, he made things that were good" [bonus est . . . et inuidens nulli, fecit quae bona sunt]; the improvement seems to suggest direct access to *Timaeus* through further study of Plato.[10]

Likewise from Catholic Rome came what may well have been the most successful and the most influential rendering of Plato's *Timaeus* ever produced, that of "Boethius, the last Roman—the first scholastic,"[11] in the first quarter of the sixth century. Boethius, too, played a prominent role in the history of the development of the doctrine of the Trinity, through his five theological tractates; "today," as Henry Chadwick has said, "it is accepted by all scholars who have given attention to the subject that the careful Neoplatonic logician who, in the first three and fifth tractates,

---

6. Waszink 1964, 77 n.
7. Johannes Mewaldt in *PW* s.v. "Lucretius (Carus)."
8. Ogilvie 1978, 15–16.
9. Lact. *Inst.* 1.8.1; Pl. *Ti.* 28C; Nock 1962; Ogilvie 1978, 79.
10. Lact. *Epit.* 64.5, 63.1–2; Pl. *Ti.* 29E; Pichon 1901, 156–57.
11. Grabmann 1909, 1:148–78; Courcelle 1967, 7.

seeks to unravel logical tangles in the usage of the Church, is none other
than the author of the *Consolation* and of the commentaries on Aristotle."[12] His translation of *Timaeus* was not the rendering that he had
envisioned when he expressed his ambition to turn all of Aristotle and
then all of Plato from Greek into Latin, "to bring them into harmony, and
to demonstrate that they do not disagree on everything, as many maintain, but are in the greatest possible agreement on many things that pertain to philosophy."[13] Although he was prevented from fulfilling this
ambition both by its sheer enormity and by his untimely death, so that all
he completed were several works of Aristotle (chiefly those dealing with
logic), one surviving fragment of Plato, who is in some respects "the
philosopher *par excellence*" in the *Consolation*,[14] is sufficient to make
posterity lament that he did not carry off the entire assignment, especially
when the elegance of its Latin is compared with the translation of
Calcidius: the twenty-eight line "Hymn to the Creator," "the great Timaean hymn" that stands "at the structural center of the *Consolation*," in
book 3, and that begins with the words "O qui perpetua mundum ratione
gubernas," is based on the central portion of *Timaeus* (27C–42D), with
borrowings from other sources both classical and Christian.[15] It may well
have done more than any other version, even including the original, to
disseminate the thought of *Timaeus* in the West.[16]

This examination of the counterpoint between *Timaeus* and *Genesis* in
Catholic Rome, then, consists of a close explication de texte of the "Hymn
to the Creator," as illuminated by the other writings of Boethius, in which,
as he acknowledged, he drew on "the seeds of argument sown in my mind
by St. Augustine's writings."[17] Much of the context and content for the
examination is therefore provided by Augustine's *On the Trinity*, *Confessions*, and *City of God*, because, as J.C.M. van Winden has observed, "the
most complete enumeration of the interpretations given to Genesis 1,1 is
found in Augustine's *Confessions*, Book XII";[18] also considered are the

---

12. Chadwick 1981, 174.
13. Boet. *Herm. sec.* 2 pr.
14. Courcelle 1967, 22.
15. Astell 1994, 46; Boet. *Cons.* 3M9.1–28. See Scheible 1972, 101–12; Gruber 1978,
277–90; Chadwick 1981, 233–35; O'Daly 1991, 163–65.
16. Courcelle 1967, 177–84, 432; Chenu 1968, 49–98; Troncarelli 1987.
17. Boet. *Trin.* pr.; on the question of Augustine's place in relation to the *Consolation*,
see Silk 1939 and, above all, Chadwick 1981, 174–222.
18. Winden 1973, 377. See also Aimé Solignac in Vignaux 1973, 153–71.

several commentaries of Augustine on *Genesis,* works of Hilary and Ambrose, and the commentary of Calcidius on *Timaeus.* Ambrose, Augustine, and Boethius—and probably Calcidius if he was a colleague of Ossius—listened to *Genesis,* to *Timaeus,* and to the counterpoint between the two works through a Trinitarian filter. In this way Philo's innovative equating of the one Creator God Almighty of *Genesis* with the ποιητὴς καὶ πατήρ of *Timaeus*[19] could be carried over into the equating of that one Creator God with the Trinity, as in the formula of the Council of Nicaea (which was reported in Latin by Hilary of Poitiers):[20] "Credimus in unum deum patrem omnipotentem [omnium] uisibilium et inuisibilium factorem. . . . Et in unum dominum Iesum Christum. . . . Et in spiritum sanctum."[21] In keeping with his "regula canonica" about the Trinitarian interpretation of Scripture,[22] Augustine applied to these three divine Persons and this one divine Substance in the Trinity the plural as well as the singular in the words of *Romans* 11:36: "Source, Guide, and Goal of all that is—to him be glory for ever!" [Ex ipso et per ipsum et in ipso sunt omnia; ipsi gloria in saecula saeculorum!][23]

Philosophy and Traditional Religion

As those references to the dogma of the Trinity indicate, one of the massive differences between a philosopher of classical Rome such as Lucretius and a philosopher of Catholic Rome such as Boethius lay in their handling of the relation between philosophy and traditional religion. Already in the preamble to the "Hymn to the Creator," therefore, the statement in Plato's *Timaeus* that "all men who possess even a share of good sense call upon God [θεὸν καλοῦσιν] always at the outset of every undertaking, be it small or great,"[24] whatever may have been its original intention, became an authoritative proof text that Philosophia quoted expressly to Boethius and to which she obtained his no less express assent, employing the language of *Timaeus:* "We must call upon the Father of all things [rerum omnium patrem], for if this is omitted no beginning can be rightly and properly based."[25] In such passages, as Helga Scheible has put it, "the

---

19. Pl. *Ti.* 29C.

20. On Hilary's importance for Augustine's Trinitarian thought, see Aug. *Trin.* 10.10.11.

21. Tanner-Alberigo 1:5.

22. Pelikan 1990.

23. Aug. *Trin.* 1.6.12.

24. Pl. *Ti.* 27B–C.

25. Boet. *Cons.* 3P9.32–33.

blending of the Creator of the world (here, that of the Old Testament) with the Supreme Idea of Platonism makes it possible for the Christian thinker to find an adequate way of speaking about his God."[26] Calcidius, too, as was his wont, made his translation of this passage into an extended paraphrase, with an appeal to universal tradition: "It is customary for all, as a kind of religious duty, . . . to pray to the Deity for help" [cum omnibus mos sit et quasi quaedam religio . . . precari ad auxilium diuinitatem].[27] As the summary conclusion to his *Consolation of Philosophy*, Boethius insisted: "Nor vainly are our hopes placed in God, nor our prayers, which when they are right, cannot be ineffectual."[28] In agreement with Augustine's commentary on *Genesis*,[29] as well as with other writers, a clinching argument that Boethius drew from the philosophical discussion of providence, foreknowledge, and fate was the same *reductio ad absurdum*, that if determinism were correct, there would be "no sense in hoping for anything, or in praying that anything may be averted."[30] This argument of Boethius was at the same time an assertion of the confidence in "Reason controlling Necessity [ἀνάγκη]" celebrated in *Timaeus*,[31] where "necessary causes" were seen as "subservient causes" [αἰτίαις ὑπηρετούσαις] in contrast to "the divine" [τὸ θεῖον] and reasonable causes, which were in control for the sake of the primary cause, namely, the Good.[32] It is plausible that Boethius was, by this reductio ad absurdum, also directing a polemic against the *De rerum natura* of Lucretius, which attacked the superstitious confidence of priests and their victims in prayer and sacrifice, on the grounds that "the holy divinity" [sanctum numen] was caught captive within "the boundaries of fate" [fati finis] and therefore could not be of any help to the suppliant.[33] Therefore Boethius could conclude one of his theological tractates with a reminder of what "our Lord Jesus Christ himself taught us to desire in our prayers."[34] He began another of his theological tractates with the orthodox confession that "the surest source of all truth is admittedly the fundamental doctrines

---

26. Scheible 1972, 104.
27. Cal. *Ti.* 22.
28. Boet. *Cons.* 5P6.46.
29. Aug. *Gen. litt.* 2.17.
30. Boet. *Cons.* 5P3.33. See the parallels cited in Gruber 1978, 392.
31. Pl. *Ti.* 48A.
32. Pl. *Ti.* 68E.
33. Lucr. 5.305–10.
34. Boet. *Eut.* 8.

of the Catholic faith," and he concluded it with the imperative to "reconcile faith and reason."[35] For it was his intent in all these tractates to expound what "Catholics in accordance with reason confess" about "the middle way of the Christian Faith" and "the true and solid content of the Catholic Faith" [firma ueraque fides catholica].[36] The confidence that this content was "true and solid" enabled Augustine to expound *Genesis* "not by the method of affirmation but by that of inquiry" [non adfirmando, sed quaerendo], just as long as this method of doubting inquiry "does not exceed the limits of the Catholic faith."[37] On the basis of such a preestablished harmony between biblical faith and Greek reason, Calcidius could link the martyrdom of Socrates with those of Isaiah and Jeremiah,[38] just as Boethius could honor Socrates as a martyr.[39] For, as he declared at the conclusion of another tractate, in a summary statement of his program of faith in search of understanding, the task of his philosophical theology was to "furnish some fitting support in argument to an article which stands quite firmly by itself on the foundation of Faith."[40]

The article of faith he had in mind in those words, which had first been established by authority and was binding on that ground but which was now also to be examined by reason and philosophy, was the doctrine of the One God as Trinity; "the Trinity consists," as Boethius defined it, "in plurality of Persons, the unity in simplicity of substance."[41] On this dogma, according to Boethius, it was obligatory to adhere to "the language of the Church" [ecclesiasticus loquendi usus] and to obey "the decision of ecclesiastical usage" [ecclesiasticae locutionis arbitrium].[42] Boethius was probably making not more than a slight allusion to this doctrine when, in the *Consolation of Philosophy,* discussing the relation between sufficiency, power, and "respect" [reuerentia], he proposed that "we judge these three to be one."[43] But if, as scholars now agree, Boethius is the author of both the *Consolation* and *On the Trinity,* so that despite the notorious silence of the *Consolation* about Christianity, "the Christianising reading of the *Consolation* is one that Boethius himself

---

35. Boet. *Div.*
36. Boet. *Eut.* 6, int., 7.
37. Aug. *Gen. imp.* 1.
38. Cal. *Com.* 172.
39. Boet. *Cons.* 1P3.9.
40. Boet. *Trin.* 6.
41. Boet. *Div.* 55–57.
42. Boet. *Eut.* 3, 4.
43. Boet. *Cons.* 3P9.8; see also 3M9.13.

makes possible by the way in which he writes the book,"[44] it is an attractive application of "the language of the Church" to identify the "everlasting reason" [perpetua ratio] in the opening line of the "Hymn to the Creator," as well as the "divine reason" [diuina ratio] to which according to an earlier prose passage of the *Consolation* the governance of the world was subject and which was synonymous with "providence,"[45] with the divine and everlasting "ratio" or λόγος, the Second Person of the Trinity, through whom, according to the *Gospel of John,* God had created the world.[46] Reciting the Trinitarian creed at the beginning of *De Trinitate,* Augustine affirmed, "And this is my faith because this is the Catholic faith" [Haec et mea fides est quando haec est catholica fides].[47] After a similar recital at the beginning of his early commentary on *Genesis* (although with a somewhat variant text of the creed), he declared this to be what "Catholic discipline commands that we believe" and follow in the interpretation of *Genesis.*[48] Even without such a command, he followed it also in the interpretation of *Timaeus.* Augustine invoked the passage in *Timaeus* that distinguished between Truth (ἀλήθεια) and Belief (πίστις), according to which Truth pertained only to Being (οὐσία) but not to Becoming (γένεσις).[49] He called the distinction "certainly a valid statement" [profecto uera sententia] and applied it to Christ as Truth and as "eternity," who had referred to knowing the Trinity when he said, "This is eternal life: to know thee who alone art truly God, and Jesus Christ, whom thou hast sent."[50] That passage from *Timaeus* was, with others, evidence for the truth of the statement of Paul that the "invisible attributes" of God were "visible in the things he has made," but it was also evidence for the inadequacy of "philosophizing without the Mediator, that is, without Christ the man."[51] Thus in Christian New Rome and in Catholic Rome, the familiar warning of *Timaeus,* "To discover the Maker and Father of this Universe were a task indeed; and having discovered Him, to declare

---

44. Chadwick 1981, 222. Many long-standing questions on this issue have been laid to rest by Chadwick's book, which, as Lerer (1985, 10) observes, "successfully establishes [Boethius's] place in early church history."

45. Boet. *Cons.* 1P6.20, 4P6.9. On providence, see Ambr. *Hex.* 3.17.71 and Scheible 1972, 184–87.

46. *Jn.* 1:3, knowable also by reason (Aug. *Conf.* 7.9.13–14).

47. Aug. *Trin.* 1.5.7.

48. Aug. *Gen. imp.* 1.

49. Pl. *Ti.* 29C–D; Cic. *Ti.* 3.8.

50. Aug. *Trin.* 4.18.24; *Jn.* 17:3.

51. Aug. *Trin.* 13.19.24, quoting *Rom.* 1:20 and 1 *Tm.* 2:5.

Him unto all men were a thing impossible,"[52] had been quoted over and over again in opposition to polytheism (for example, by Justin Martyr, Minucius Felix, Tertullian, Clement of Alexandria, and Eusebius) and would go on proving to be useful.[53]

But because, conversely, "in our Mediator are hidden all the treasures of wisdom and of knowledge," as the protection both against the seductiveness of "false philosophy" and against the terrors of "the superstition of false religion," thus in a polemical double stroke both against the materialistic philosophy that Lucretius had espoused and against the pagan superstition that he had attacked,[54] there could also be an authentic wisdom and a true philosophy, celebrated by Plato as the love of God.[55] Plato's teaching that "philosophers must involve themselves in political affairs" had induced Boethius to "apply in the practice of public administration what I learned from [philosophy] in the seclusion of my private leisure," for it was God himself who had "set [philosophy] in the minds of philosophers."[56] The supreme embodiment of Plato's ideal of the philosopher-king had been Solomon, the king who was a philosopher and the inspired writer of four philosophical books of the Bible.[57] Therefore "the identification of the Boethian Philosophia with the Biblical Wisdom" became a common practice among medieval readers of the *Consolation.*[58] They read the personified Philosophia who spoke in Boethius's *Consolation of Philosophy* in the light of the personified Sophia who spoke in Solomon's *Book of Proverbs* and *Book of Wisdom,* which had in turn been taken by Calcidius to be in agreement with the claim in Plato's *Timaeus* that Sophia had been present at the creation.[59] Such an identification would seem all the more plausible because of Philosophia's direct quotation from *Wisdom* 8:1, in which, Boethius said, "not only the conclusion, the sum of your arguments, delight me, but much more the very words you use [multo magis haec ipsa quibus uteris uerba]," presumably because they came directly from the Bible.[60] Accordingly, Augustine re-

---

52. Pl. *Ti.* 28C; Cic. *Ti.* 2.6.

53. Nock 1962, 79–86; see the partial catalog in Geffcken 1907, 174–75.

54. Aug. *Gen. litt.* 1.21; *Col.* 2:8.

55. Aug. *Civ.* 8.11.

56. Boet. *Cons.* 1P4.6–8; cf. Pl. *Ti.* 47A–E.

57. Ambr. *Exc. Sat.* 2.30–31.

58. Troncarelli 1987, 113.

59. Cal. *Com.* 276.

60. Boet. *Cons.* 3P12.63–68; *Wis.* 8:1. Chadwick (1982, 237–38) points out that this biblical reference "enforces a doctrine of natural theology, not revealed."

peatedly utilized *Wisdom* as the key to *Genesis,* including that same passage, *Wisdom* 8:1, to interpret *Genesis* 1:24–25.[61] Both Sophia and Philosophia spoke with a divine authority, inspiring "awe."[62] Philosophia had the authority and ability, according to Boethius, "to unfurl the causes of hidden things [latentium rerum causas euoluere] and to unfold explanations veiled in mist."[63] She urged human reason to press as far as its limits would permit, but she admonished that it was "most just that human reason should submit to the divine mind."[64] That dual function of reason made the practice of philosophy and the adherence to traditional Trinitarian orthodoxy, and hence the interpretation of *Timaeus* and the interpretation of *Genesis,* neither identical nor incompatible.

Creator of Heaven and Earth

The hymn of Boethius was addressed to the "Creator of heaven and earth" [terrarum caelique sator], celebrated in the next book as "artifex."[65] The designation "heaven and earth" was shared by *Genesis* and other cosmogonies, including that of Lucretius, and was, Augustine saw, a synonym for "universe."[66] An earlier hymn in the *Consolation* was addressed to the "Maker of the circle of the stars, / Seated on your eternal throne, / Spinner of the whirling heavens, / Binding the constellations by your law";[67] and a later hymn praised "the Maker of this great universe [magni conditor orbis]. . . . / What is, what has been, and what is to come, / In one swift mental stab he sees."[68] In a direct echo of the statement of "the supreme originating principle of Becoming and the Cosmos" in *Timaeus*—that God "was good, and in him that is good no envy ariseth ever concerning anything"[69]—and also in an echo of *Genesis* as it had come to be read,[70] Philosophia, paraphrasing an Augustinian argument (and anticipating the Anselmic ontological argument), asserted, "That God, the principle of all things, is good is proved by the common concept of all men's minds; for since nothing better than God can be conceived of,

61. Aug. *Gen. litt.* 3.12; Aug. *Gen. imp.* 15.
62. Boet. *Cons.* 1P1.1.
63. Boet. *Cons.* 4P6.1, apparently an echo of Lucr. 5.774–75.
64. Boet. *Cons.* 5P5.11.
65. Boet. *Cons.* 3M9.2, 4P6.12. See Lerer 1985, 208 nn.
66. Aug. *Gen. litt.* 5.2; cf. Pl. *Ti.* 28B and Waszink 1964, 56–57.
67. Boet. *Cons.* 1M5.1–4.
68. Boet. *Cons.* 5M2 7, 11–12.
69. Pl. *Ti.* 29D–E; Cic. *Ti.* 3.9.
70. Phil. *Opif.* 21.

who can doubt that that, than which nothing is better, is good?"[71] For, as Augustine had summarized both cosmogonies, "Because God is both omnipotent [*Genesis*] and good [*Timaeus*], he made all things to be altogether good [*Genesis* and *Timaeus*]."[72]

Elsewhere Augustine strove to harmonize *Timaeus* and *Genesis* on this point. He drew a direct parallel between the repeated refrain of *Genesis*, "God saw that it was good,"[73] and the formula of *Timaeus* that "when the Father that engendered it perceived it in motion and alive, a thing of joy to the eternal gods, He too rejoiced."[74] Commenting on these words of *Timaeus*, he added, "Plato too was not, when he said this, so foolish as to suppose that God's happiness was made greater by surprise at his new creation"; to the contrary, Plato "merely wished to show by his words that the work won the approval of the artist as much when finished [iam factum] as when it was but a design for skilful execution [in arte faciendum]."[75] In *Timaeus* Plato had said that there were three questions, "the Becoming, that 'Wherein' it becomes, and the source 'Wherefrom' the Becoming is copied and produced" [τὸ μὲν γιγνόμενον, τὸ δ! ἐν ᾧ γίγνεται, τὸ δ! ὅθεν ἀφομοιούμενον φύεται τὸ γιγνόμενον].[76] It was formally similar but substantively quite different when Augustine raised three questions or "three chief matters concerning a work of creation that had to be reported to us and that it behoved us to know, namely who made it, by what means, and why." All three were answered in the single verse "God said, 'Let there be light'; and there was light. And God saw that the light was good."[77] To the three questions, therefore, *Genesis* answered: "So if we ask, 'Who made it?' the answer is 'It was God.' If we ask, 'By what means?' the answer is 'God said, "Let it be"; and it was.' If we ask, 'Why?' the answer is 'Because it is good.'" Although both *Genesis* and *Timaeus* were in agreement on this point that the world was "good," *Timaeus*, not *Genesis*, in so many words had made this "goodness" an answer to Augustine's question of "why," when it identified this as "the Cause wherefor He that constructed it constructed Becoming and the All: He was good, and in him that is good no envy ariseth ever concerning anything;

71. Boet. *Cons.* 3P.10.7.
72. Aug. *Gen. litt.* 4.16.
73. *Gn.* 1:4, 10, 12, 18, 21, 25, 30.
74. Pl. *Ti.* 37C; according to Giomini 1975, 228, Augustine is not quoting from Cicero's translation here.
75. Aug. *Civ.* 11.21; cf. Ambr. *Hex.* 2.5.19–21.
76. Pl. *Ti.* 50C.
77. *Gn.* 1:3.

and being devoid of envy He desired that all should be, as far as possible, like unto Himself."[78] Augustine immediately went on to link the testimony of Plato's *Timaeus* with this exegesis of *Genesis:* "Plato too gives this as the proper reason, beyond all other reasons, for the world's creation, namely, that good works might be created by a good God."[79] In attempting to account for this striking harmony between *Genesis* and *Timaeus,* Augustine considered several possible explanations, without making a specific choice between them at this point:

> He [Plato] may have read our passage, or may have got knowledge of it from those who had read it, or else by his superlatively keen insight [acerrimo ingenio] he gained "vision of the unseen truths of God through understanding of God's creation," or he too may have learned of these truths from such men as had gained vision of them.[80]

That harmonization between *Timaeus* and *Genesis* was in keeping with the Catholic way, which, according to Boethius, was to "reconcile faith and reason."[81]

In an earlier treatment by Augustine of the relation between *Timaeus* and *Genesis* there were likewise three such issues for reconciliation.[82] Quoting the opening verses of *Genesis,* he found that the parallels with *Timaeus* had been strong enough to give rise to the theory of various Jewish and Christian thinkers that Plato had read the *Genesis* cosmogony. Augustine's answer to this theory was to argue on the basis of chronology, here in book 8 of the *City of God,* that Plato could not have heard the prophet Jeremiah or had access to the Septuagint *Genesis;* he modified this somewhat in book 11.[83] But he did not seek in either passage to demonstrate from a comparison of the two texts how dissonant they were. On the contrary, as he examined another chronology, that of the creation narrative in *Genesis* 1, he took the words of *Genesis* 2, "This is the book of the creation of heaven and earth, when the day was made" [Hic est liber creaturae caeli et terrae, cum factus est dies], to mean that the six days were intended to refer not to six discrete periods of time but to the estab-

---

78. Pl. *Ti.* 29D–E.
79. Pl. *Ti.* 28A; Cic. *Ti.* 3.9.
80. Aug. *Civ.* 11.21, quoting *Rom.* 1:20.
81. Boet. *Div.*
82. Aug. *Civ.* 8.11.
83. Aug. *Civ.* 11.21.

lishment of cosmic order.[84] Although the six days were not literal days and God had "created all things simultaneously," the creation recounted in the hexaemeron was "nevertheless not therefore without order."[85] The idea of cosmic order was not alien to the *Genesis* account, particularly with the use of the term κόσμος in the Septuagint;[86] nevertheless, the centrality of the concept of order, and therefore the substitution of order for chronology as an explanation of why *Genesis* spoke of six days of creation, was evidence not for Plato's having read *Genesis* but for Augustine's having read *Timaeus,* with its declaration that the Creator, "when he took over all that was visible, seeing that it was not in a state of rest but in a state of discordant and disorderly motion, brought it into order out of disorder."[87]

A second point of contact between the two cosmogonies, according to Augustine, was the theory of the four elements.[88] The catalog of the elements from *Timaeus* in *Wisdom*[89] provided Augustine with a justification for repeatedly invoking the elements in his exegesis of *Genesis*.[90] It was a Catholic consensus concerning "the followers of Plato" that "the Hebrews agree with them" as regards the distinction between the "rational soul" [anima rationabilis] and "matter" [silua].[91] The *Book of Wisdom* had, moreover, spoken of God's having "created the world out of formless matter" [κτίσασα τὸν κόσμον ἐξ ἀμόρφου ὕλης], a statement that seemed to be based on *Timaeus*.[92] According to Augustine in all three of his commentaries on *Genesis*, however, this "formless matter" could not be said to have been uncreated, and both it and the things that had form had been created simultaneously, the priority of the formless matter being a matter "not of time, but of origin."[93] The "formless matter" of the *Book of Wisdom* was not exempted from the all-inclusive paraphrase of the first two chapters of *Genesis* by the prologue to the *Gospel of John:* "All things were made through him," the Logos.[94]

---

84. *Gn.* 2:4; Aug. *Gen. litt.* 5.1.
85. Aug. *Gen. litt.* 3.32–33.
86. *Gn.* 2:1.
87. Pl. *Ti.* 30A.
88. Pl. *Ti.* 31B, 32B; Ambr. *Hex.* 1.8.30.
89. *Wis.* 13:2.
90. Aug. *Gen. imp.* 4; Aug. *Gen. litt.* 2.3. See Pépin 1964, 432–33.
91. Cal. *Com.* 300; cf. Switalski 1902, 45–48.
92. *Wis.* 11:17; Pl. *Ti.* 50D–51A.
93. Aug. *Gen. Man.* 1.7.11–12; Aug. *Gen. imp.* 3; Aug. *Gen. litt.* 1.14–15.
94. Aug. *Gen. litt.* 5.17; *Jn.* 1:3.

That same passage enabled Catholic exegesis, in its treatment of the question "From what did God create the world?" to draw on another of the component ideas of Plato's metaphysics, the doctrine of Forms, as it had appeared also in *Timaeus*. For the words in *John* meant that "the very Wisdom of God [ipsa Dei sapientia], through whom all things were made, knew those divine, unchangeable, eternal reasons even before they were made."[95] This passage likewise implied that the angels, as "the chief creatures" [principaliter conditi], had also known the Forms or "eternal reasons" of the entire created universe in that very Word of God.[96] Thus the light referred to by the opening words of God in creation preexisted "in the Word of God according to reason, that is, in the coeternal Wisdom of God," and only afterward came into existence in the realm of nature.[97] The omnipotence of God the Creator, which, Augustine said on the basis of *Timaeus*, "according to Plato, preserves both things that had a beginning from perishing and things that were bound together from disintegrating,"[98] was manifested in the resurrection of the body. For, as Augustine continued on the basis of *Timaeus*, "the lesser gods, who were charged by Plato with the creation of man as well as of the other terrestrial animals were able, as he declares, to remove from fire the property of burning, while leaving that of brightness to flash through the eyes."[99] Arguing from *Timaeus* but for a distinctive teaching of Scripture and the church, Augustine concluded, "If then the will and power of the supreme God can [do all of this], as Plato himself has allowed, . . . shall we hesitate to allow him to abolish putrefaction of the flesh of any man on whom he bestows immortality, while leaving the properties intact, and to retain the harmony of design among its members [congruentiam figurae membrorumque], while removing the sluggishness of its weight?"[100]

The third and most striking point of harmony that Augustine found between *Genesis* and *Timaeus*—a point so striking that he acknowledged it "brings me virtually to an admission that Plato was not without knowledge of those books" of Moses, just as also elsewhere he admitted the possibility that Plato "may have read" *Genesis*[101]—was a continuation of

---

95. Aug. *Gen. litt.* 5.13; see Wolfson 1956, 282–83.

96. Aug. *Gen. litt.* 4.24.

97. Aug. *Gen. litt.* 2.8.

98. Pl. *Ti.* 41A–B.

99. Pl. *Ti.* 45B; according to Giomini 1975, 228, Augustine is not quoting from Cicero's translation here.

100. Aug. *Civ.* 13.18.

101. Aug. *Civ.* 11.21.

the process by which the God of Moses had come to be seen as the ὁ ὤν of Plato, as a result of which there was a clear agreement between Plato's doctrine of Being and the self-manifestation of God to Moses from the burning bush: "I am the One who am" [Ego sum qui sum].[102] By drawing the ontological distinction between the Creator and all creatures, the creation narrative in the First Book of Moses necessarily implied that when this divine self-manifestation in the Second Book of Moses used the verb "to be," it was intended "in a vastly different sense" [longe aliter] from the way it was used when it was applied to any creature.[103] The difference consisted in this: "God is οὐσία or essence, for he is and is especially that from which proceeds the being of all things. He is οὐσίωσις, i.e., subsistence."[104] The general metaphysical principle that "being and unity are convertible terms, and whatever is one, is" [esse enim atque unum conuertitur et quodcumque unum est, est], while applicable also to other doctrines,[105] applied preeminently to the being of God and also to the being of God as Trinity. This biblical doctrine of Being was at the same time a "tenet [which] Plato strenuously upheld and most earnestly urged upon others." But Augustine added that he did not know "whether this statement can be found anywhere in the writings of those who preceded Plato," except of course in the word from the burning bush itself.[106]

Such a clarification of the verb "to be" was indispensable in Catholic language about the Trinity, as Boethius explained when in the prolegomena to his *De Trinitate* he provided the definition that God "is very being and the source of being" [esse ipsum est et ex qua esse est] and that therefore "the divine substance" [diuina substantia] was pure form.[107] But this had to be defined even more precisely, because although "substantia" was the first among the "ten categories which can be universally predicated of all things," it could be applied to God only if it was specified that "substance in Him is not really substantial but supersubstantial" [substantia in illo non est uere substantia sed ultra substantiam],[108] so that the normal language of affirmation did not properly apply to transcendent reality. The incorporation of "substance" or "being" as οὐσία into the ὁμοούσιος of the Creed of Nicaea, together with the distinction

---

102. *Ex.* 3:14.
103. Aug. *Gen. litt.* 5.16.
104. Boet. *Eut.* 3.
105. Boet. *Eut.* 4.
106. Aug. *Civ.* 8.11.
107. Boet. *Trin.* 2.
108. Boet. *Trin.* 4.

between the one οὐσία of the Godhead and the three ὑποστάσεις of Father, Son, and Holy Spirit, meant that the "ecclesiasticus loquendi usus" was permeated with the vocabulary of Trinitarian ontology, in the Greek of New Rome and also in the Latin of Catholic Rome, even though the relation between the Greek and the Latin vocabulary was sometimes a source of confusion.[109]

The Order of Creation

From the understanding of "being" as properly belonging to God the Creator alone, and only derivatively to the creation, an important corollary necessarily followed. "That is, which keeps its order" [Est enim quod ordinem retinet].[110] As both *Timaeus* and *Genesis*, when read together, defined creation as "bringing order out of disorder,"[111] so, too, they both celebrated the order of creation. In the words of the "Hymn to the Creator," "Thou, height of beauty, in Thy mind the beauteous world / Dost bear, and in that ideal likeness shaping it, / Dost order perfect parts a perfect whole to frame" [Pulchrum pulcherrimus ipse / Mundum mente gerens similique in imagine formans / Perfectasque iubens perfectum absoluere partes].[112] So all-pervasive was this order of creation that even "that which has departed from the rule of this order appointed to it, although it slips into another condition yet that too is order, so that nothing in the realm of providence may be left to chance."[113] In *Genesis* God divided light from darkness (which Augustine had learned through his conflict with Manichaeism to define negatively, or privatively, as the absence of light, not positively as a reality on its own), so that "even these privations [of reality] might have an order of their own"; for "God is not the author of our faults, but he is the orderer of them."[114] For the sake of order, creation was narrated chronologically, even though it had taken place simultaneously.

Within the created world, the primary modality of order was time: as "Creator of the planets and the sky," God had brought "time from timelessness."[115] Therefore time could be defined by Calcidius as "the sim-

---

109. Aug. *Trin.* 5.8.10.
110. Boet. *Cons.* 4P2.36, 4P4.27.
111. Pl. *Ti.* 30A.
112. Boet. *Cons.* 3M9.7–9.
113. Boet. *Cons.* 4P6.53.
114. Aug. *Gen. Man.* 1.4.7; Aug. *Gen. imp.* 5.
115. Boet. *Cons.* 3M9.2–3.

ulacrum of eternity."[116] Both *Genesis* and *Timaeus,* each in its own way, had referred to this creation of time.[117] But that reference of *Genesis* to the creation of the heavenly bodies on the fourth day for the purpose of measuring time could not be taken to mean that there had been no time before.[118] Time, too, had been created, as had the angels; and time began with creation.[119] The reference of *Timaeus* to an existence of the world before time likewise needed, according to Boethius, to be interpreted correctly:

> Therefore those are not right who, when they hear that Plato thought this world neither had a beginning in time nor would have an end, think that in this way the created world is made co-eternal with the Creator. For it is one thing to be drawn out through a life without bounds, which is what Plato attributes to the world, but it is a different thing to have embraced at once the whole presence of boundless life, which it is clear is the property of the divine mind. Nor should God seem to be more ancient than created things by some amount of time, but rather by his own simplicity of nature.[120]

As Boethius argued elsewhere, to say that God "ever is" [semper est] meant that for God this "ever" had to be taken as "a term of present time," an eternal Now, "abiding, unmoved, and immovable," which could not be true of the world.[121]

In opposition to those who "have regard not to the order of the world but their own desires" and who as a result "think the freedom to commit evil and go unpunished for the evil done is a happy thing," it needed to be emphasized that the order of creation implied the divine moral order.[122] Therefore the prayer in the "Hymn to the Creator" for "light" to "disperse the clouds of earthly matter's cloying weight," so that the creatures of God could "fix on Thee our mind's unblinded eye,"[123] was a petition not only for the mind to receive intellectual illumination but for the will to attain moral integrity. The direct correlation between the two

116. Cal. *Com.* 23; Ladner 1959, 211 n. 34; Pépin 1964, 156 n. 1.
117. *Gn.* 1:14–19; Pl. *Ti.* 39C; Cic. *Ti.* 9.32–34.
118. Aug. *Gen. litt.* 2.14.
119. Aug. *Gen. imp.* 3; Aug. *Gen. litt.* 5.5.
120. Boet. *Cons.* 5P6.9–11. Gruber 1978, 409–10, cites the parallel of Aug. *Civ.* 11.4; also appropriate is Ambr. *Hex.* 1.1.3.
121. Boet. *Trin.* 4.
122. Boet. *Cons.* 4P4.27.
123. Boet. *Cons.* 3M9.23–25.

divine acts of creating the human race and of issuing a moral "charge" to the human race was central to the cosmogony of *Genesis,* as well as to the outcome of the cosmogony in the narrative of the fall, but it was not nearly so central to the account of human origins in *Timaeus.* For the latter, the closest parallel to the "charge" of God to Adam came rather in the charge issued by the Demiurge, as their "framer and father," to the lesser gods.[124] The description of the Demiurge in the cosmogony of Plato as the "framer and father" [opifex paterque], terminology that had by now been transferred to the Creator in the cosmogony of Moses, meant that as "framer" the Demiurge was the one who had made them but that as "father" he made provision for them to attain beatitude by commanding them to obey the moral order of his will.[125] In his commentary on this passage, Calcidius explained the words addressed by the Demiurge to the lesser gods according to Plato in the light of "the prohibition addressed by God to our first parents according to Moses," one of whose most important implications was the doctrine of free will, which taught that "the power to abstain or not to abstain [from eating the forbidden fruit] resided with them"; for "if it had been by necessity that this was to happen, it would have been in vain for him to prohibit it."[126]

The most important expression of this correlation between the divine order and the moral order was the doctrine of creation in the image of God. In accordance with a tradition going back to Alexandria, the thinkers of Catholic Rome continued the definition of the image of God as rationality, thus supplying a concept that they derived from Jerusalem and *Genesis* with a content that they derived from Athens and *Timaeus.*[127] But they pressed this traditional combination considerably further, extending the teaching of *Genesis* about the creation of humanity in accordance with the image of God to include the teaching of *Timaeus* about the creation of the universe in accordance with a model that was eternal.[128] For the entire cosmos shared in the image of God, as Plato had taught in the often repeated axiom of *Timaeus* that "If so be that this Cosmos is beautiful and its Constructor good, it is plain that he fixed his gaze on the Eternal."[129] Thus the doctrine of the image and likeness of God was applied to the entire universe, and God's "ideal likeness" was said to

124. Pl. *Ti.* 41A–B; Cic. *Ti.* 11.40–41.
125. Cal. *Com.* 139.
126. Cal. *Com.* 154.
127. Aug. *Gen. imp.* 16.
128. *Gn.* 1:27; Pl. *Ti.* 29B; Cic. *Ti.* 2.7.
129. Pl. *Ti.* 29A; Cic. *Ti.* 2.6.

"turn the firmament in similar patterns."[130] Yet Ambrose and Augustine preserved the original point of the biblical doctrine, which had been to emphasize, also morally, the distinctiveness of the human race as protected from desecration by the holiness of the God who had made it in his own image.[131] Like the doctrine of creation itself, the doctrine of the creation of man in the image of God was at the same time eschatological in its implications, looking backward to the quality that had originally set humanity apart from all other creatures, but also carrying with it the promise of a destiny that was no less distinctive. Philosophia put it to Boethius as "a kind of corollary":

> Since men are made happy by the acquisition of happiness, but happiness is itself divinity, it is obvious that they are made happy by the acquisition of divinity. But as by the acquisition of justice they become just, or by the acquisition of wisdom, wise, so by the same argument they must, when they have acquired divinity, become gods. Therefore every happy man is a god, though by nature God is one only: but nothing prevents there being as many as you like by participation.[132]

By asserting monotheism and asserting a "divinization freed of all Stoic pantheism,"[133] this extrapolation from the doctrine of creation in the image of God was a summary of the definition of salvation as θέωσις, which, while not absent from the tradition of Western Latin Christianity, was more central to the spirituality and theology of the Greek Christian East.

It was largely a Western Latin innovation when the image of God became, in the thought of Augustine, a creation in the image of the Trinity and therefore a Trinitarian image. The plurals in the phrase of *Genesis,* "Let us make man in our image and likeness" had somehow to be squared with biblical monotheism. Already in the first Christian dialogue with Judaism after the New Testament to have been preserved, these words had functioned as proof that the Son of God, "who was truly brought forth from the Father, was with the Father before all creatures."[134] The argu-

---

130. Boet. *Cons.* 3M9.8, 17.
131. *Jas.* 3:9; Ambr. *Hex.* 6.8.47–48; Aug. *Gen. imp.* 16.
132. Boet. *Cons.* 3P10.23–25; for classical antecedents, see Gruber 1978, 295.
133. Faller 1925, 428.
134. Just. *Dial.* 52.

ment that these plurals "reveal that there is neither one isolated God, nor yet one God in two dissimilar persons," continued to be prominent in the theologies of Catholic Rome, such as those of Hilary of Poitiers and Ambrose of Milan.[135] But Augustine pressed the concept of the image, in the light of the words of *Genesis,* to make it an image of the Trinity. Already in the commentary on *Genesis* that he began and then dropped in 393, he was saying that "man was created after the image of the Trinity itself."[136] But in his theological masterpiece, the fifteen books of *De Trinitate,* he developed this insight into a speculative tour de force. The foundation of the insight was his quest for "a trinity, not any trinity, but that Trinity which is God, and the true and supreme and only God [illam trinitatem quae deus est, uerusque ac summus ac solus deus]."[137] Once found, that divine Trinity yielded an understanding of its image in the human mind, which in book 10 Augustine perceived in the relation between "these three, memory, understanding, and will" [tria haec, memoriam, intellegentiam, uoluntatem],[138] as well as in other "footsteps of the Trinity" [vestigia Trinitatis], which he traced and compared. But to make this point, Augustine had to attack those philosophers—including Cicero in the *Hortensius,* the treatise, now lost, to which Augustine attributed a major role in his own conversion[139]—who took seriously the possibility that the soul might be corporeal.[140] Returning therefore to a fuller refutation of Cicero on this point in book 14, he based his argumentation on the *Timaeus* of Plato,[141] *Timaeus* being the very treatise that Cicero had translated into Latin enabling Augustine to read it, and Plato being chief among those whom Cicero (and Augustine) called "the philosophers that were the greatest and by far the most celebrated [maximis longeque clarissimis]."[142] And when Augustine attributed the title "love" [amor] to the Holy Spirit, as a result of which what the apostle had called "the unity which the Spirit gives" applied originally and ontologically to the Trinity itself and derivatively to creatures,[143] he may also have been alluding to *Timaeus,* according to which love or "Amity" [φιλία] enabled the cosmos

135. Hil. *Trin.* 4.17–18, 3.23; Ambr. *Hex.* 6.7.41–43; Ambr. *Fid.* 1.7.51.
136. Aug. *Gen. imp.* 16.
137. Aug. *Trin.* 9.1.1.
138. Aug. *Trin.* 10.11.17–18.
139. Aug. *Conf.* 4.4.7; 8.7.17.
140. Aug. *Trin.* 10.7.9–10.
141. Pl. *Ti.* 42–43; Cic. *Ti.* 12.44–13.48.
142. Aug. *Trin.* 14.19.26.
143. *Eph.* 4:3; Aug. *Trin.* 6.5.7; Studer 1995, 577–79.

to be "united in identity with itself [and] indissoluble by any agent other than Him who had bound it together."[144]

The doctrine of the Trinity could perform this function of explaining creation, providence, and eschatology because God was, according to *Romans* 11:36, "Source, Guide, and Goal of all that is." The Trinitarian interpretation of *Romans* 11:36 had been attacked by Arius and his associates[145] and had been defended by, among others, Augustine's mentors and sources of knowledge about the Trinitarian theology of New Rome, Ambrose and Hilary, in painstaking textual analyses.[146] Augustine himself did not always interpret the passage in an explicitly Trinitarian way in his commentaries on *Genesis*.[147] But in *De Trinitate* he took it as a prime example of how the language of faith and of Scripture could refer both "singly to each person in triple fashion" [de singulis personis ter] and "to the Trinity itself not in the plural but in the singular" [de ipsa trinitate non pluraliter sed singulariter].[148] In keeping with what Boethius was to call "the middle way of the Christian Faith" and "the true and solid content of the Catholic Faith,"[149] Augustine saw the relation between singular and plural in this passage as the middle way between the error of polytheism and the error of blurring the distinctions among Father, Son, and Holy Spirit.[150] Near the beginning of his treatise, he summarized the Trinitarian exegesis of the passage:

If it is about the Father and the Son and the Holy Spirit, so as to assign each clause severally to each person [ut singulis personis singula tribuantur]—"from him," namely, from the Father; "through him," namely, through the Son; "for him," namely, for the Holy Spirit—it is manifest that the Father and the Son and the Holy Spirit is one God, inasmuch as [the apostle] continues in the singular number, "To whom be glory for ever!" [singulariter intulit: "Ipsi gloria in saecula saeculorum!"].[151]

---

144. Pl. *Ti.* 32C; Cic. *Ti.* 5.15.
145. ap. Ath. *Syn.* 16.
146. Ambr. *Fid.* 4.11.141–57; Ambr. *Hex.* 1.5.19, where it is applied to the Father; Hil. *Trin.* 8.38.
147. Aug. *Gen. imp.* 4; Aug. *Gen. litt.* 5.5, 5.13.
148. Aug. *Trin.* 5.8.9.
149. Boet. *Eut.* 6, int., 7.
150. Aug. *Trin.* 6.10.12.
151. Aug. *Trin.* 1.6.12.

And "so," as he went on to say on the basis of those words, "those three are God, one."[152]

The "Hymn to the Creator" of Boethius closed with a pleonastic apostrophe that paralleled, without the triadic formulas of that treatise or of Augustine's *De Trinitate*, "the prose-poem of the ending" of his *De fide catholica*:[153] "To see Thee is our end / Who art our source and maker, lord and path and goal" [Te cernere finis, / Principium, uector, dux, semita, terminus idem].[154] Taken together, the Pauline-Augustinian and the Boethian doxologies could be read as the cadenzas of Catholic Rome, summarizing the counterpoint of *Timaeus* and *Genesis* and at the same time responding to the questions that Lucretius had raised in classical Rome. The word meaning "source" in Boethius's hymn, *principium*, was a rendering of the term ἀρχή, which was the common property of the first sentence of part 2 of *Timaeus*, the first words of the first chapter of *Genesis*, and the first words of the *Gospel of John*;[155] by introducing it here in defense of the primacy of divine agency, Boethius was in effect rejecting the Lucretian axiom "Principium cuius hinc nobis exordia sumet, / nullam rem e nilo gigni diuinitus umquam" [The first principle of our study we will derive from this, that no thing is ever by divine agency produced out of nothing].[156] Boethius used words meaning "Guide," or "lord," and "path," *dux* and *semita*, to speak about what Philo, on the basis of both *Genesis* and *Timaeus*, had defined as the "providence that God also exercises on behalf of the cosmos" [ὅτι καὶ προνοεῖ τοῦ κόσμου ὁ θεός];[157] Boethius celebrated it here on the grounds that "nothing in the realm of providence may be left to chance."[158] He used words meaning "Goal" and "end," *terminus* and *finis*, to refer to the definition of τέλος in nature and history that *De rerum natura* had rejected (when it sought to disengage the inevitable end-as-conclusion from the notion of end-as-intention in order to posit the first while denying the second), but that *Timaeus*, against both Necessity and Chance, had declared "the supreme originating principle of Becoming and the Cosmos" [γενέσεως καὶ κόσμου . . . ἀρχὴν κυριωτάτην]. That principle was "the Cause wherefor He that constructed it constructed Becoming and the All. He was good, and in him

---

152. Aug. *Trin.* 6.5.7.
153. Chadwick 1981, 176.
154. Boet. *Cons.* 3M9.27–28.
155. Pl. *Ti.* 48A; *Gn.* 1:1; *Jn.* 1:1; Ambr. *Hex.* 1.4.12.
156. Lucr. 1.149–50.
157. Phil. *Opif.* 170–71.
158. Boet. *Cons.* 4P6.53.

that is good no envy ariseth ever concerning anything; and being devoid of envy He desired that all should be, as far as possible, like unto Himself."[159] For Catholic Rome, that principle applied, preeminently and sublimely, to the Holy Trinity as Source, Guide, and Goal.

---

159. Pl. *Ti.* 29D–E; Cic. *Ti.* 3.9.

Bibliography

Allen, Reginald E., ed. 1965. *Studies in Plato's Metaphysics*. London.

Alter, Robert. 1981. *The Art of Biblical Narrative*. New York.

Amir, Yehoshua. 1983. *Die hellenistische Gestalt des Judentums bei Philon von Alexandrien*. Neukirchen-Vluyn.

Anderson, Bernard W. 1955. "The Earth Is the Lord's: An Essay on the Biblical Doctrine of Creation." *Interpretation* 9:3–20

———. 1977. "A Stylistic Study of the Priestly Creation Story." In *Canon and Authority*, ed. George W. Coats and Burke O. Long, 148–62. Philadelphia

Andresen, Carl. 1955. *Logos und Nomos: Die Polemik des Kelsos wider das Christentum*. Berlin.

Apelt, Otto. 1922. *Platon's Dialoge "Timaios" und "Kritias" übersetzt und erläutert*. Leipzig.

Apostolopoulos, Charalambos. 1986. *Phaedo Christianus: Studien zur Verbindung und Abwägung des Verhältnisses zwischen dem platonischen "Phaidon" und dem Dialog Gregors von Nyssa "Über die Seele und die Auferstehung."* Frankfurt.

Archer-Hind, Richard Dacre. 1888. *The "Timaeus" of Plato*. London.

Armstrong, Arthur Hilary. 1948. "Platonic Elements in St. Gregory of Nyssa's Doctrine of Man." *Dominican Studies* 1:113–26.

———, ed. 1967. *The Cambridge History of Later Greek and Early Medieval Philosophy*. Cambridge.

Astell, Ann W. 1994. *Job, Boethius, and Epic Truth*. Ithaca, N.Y.

Baeumker, Clemens. 1890. *Das Problem der Materie in der griechischen Philosophie*. Münster.

Baltes, Matthias. 1976. *Die Weltentstehung des Platonischen "Timaios" nach den antiken Interpreten*. Leiden.

Bickerman, Elias. 1976. "The Septuagint as Translation." In *Studies in Jewish and Christian History*, 1:167–200. Leiden.

Bidez, Joseph. 1945. *EOS ou Platon et l'Orient*. Brussels.

Bigg, Charles. 1886. *The Christian Platonists of Alexandria*. Oxford.

Bömer, Franz. 1969. *P. Ovidius Naso "Metamorphosen": Kommentar*. Vol. 1. Heidelberg.

Bousset, Wilhelm. 1915. *Jüdisch-christlicher Schulbetrieb in Alexandria und Rom*. Göttingen.

Bowen, Alan C., ed. 1991. *Science and Philosophy in Classical Greece*. New York and London.

Bowersock, Glen Warren. 1990. *Hellenism in Late Antiquity.* Ann Arbor.

Brisson, Luc. 1974. *Le même et l'autre dans la structure ontologique du "Timée" du Platon; un commentaire systématique di "Timée" de Platon.* Paris.

Brunner, Emil. 1939. *Man in Revolt: A Christian Anthropology.* Trans. Olive Wyon. Philadelphia.

Bückers, Hermann. 1938. *Die Unsterblichkeitslehre des Weisheitsbuches.* Münster.

Burnet, John. 1928. *Platonism.* Berkeley.

Bury, Robert Gregg, ed. and trans. 1929. *Timaeus, Critias, Cleitophon, Menexenus, Epistles,* by Plato. Cambridge, Mass.

Callahan, John F. 1948. *Four Views of Time in Ancient Philosophy.* Cambridge, Mass.

———. 1958. "Greek Philosophy and the Cappadocian Cosmology." *Dumbarton Oaks Papers* 12:29–57.

Chadwick, Henry, ed. and trans. 1953. *Contra Celsum,* by Origen. Cambridge.

———. 1966. *Early Christian Thought and the Classical Tradition: Studies in Justin, Clement, and Origen.* New York.

———. 1981. *Boethius: The Consolations of Music, Logic, Theology, and Philosophy.* Oxford.

Chenu, Marie-Dominique. 1968. *Nature, Man, and Society in the Twelfth Century.* Ed. and trans. Jerome Taylor and Lester A. Little. Chicago.

Claghorn, George Stuart. 1954. *Aristotle's Criticism of Plato's "Timaeus."* The Hague.

Clark, Stephen R. L. 1984. *From Athens to Jerusalem: The Love of Wisdom and the Love of God.* Oxford.

Cochrane, Charles Norris. 1944. *Christianity and Classical Culture: A Study of Thought and Action from Augustus to Augustine.* New York and London.

Collins, John J. 1983. *Between Athens and Jerusalem.* New York.

Colpe, Carsten. 1979. "Von der Logoslehre des Philon zu der des Clemens von Alexandrien." In *Kerygma und Logos: Festschrift für C. Andresen,* ed. Adolf Martin Ritter, 89–107. Göttingen.

Conybeare, Frederick Cornwallis, and St. George Stock. 1988. *Grammar of Septuagint Greek.* 1905. Reprint, Peabody, Mass.

Cornford, Francis MacDonald. 1957. *Plato's Cosmology: The "Timaeus" of Plato Translated with a Running Commentary.* 1937. Reprint, New York.

Courcelle, Pierre. 1967. *La consolation de philosophie dans la tradition littéraire: Antécédents et postérité de Boèce.* Paris.

Courtonne, Yves. 1934. *Saint Basile et l'hellénisme: Étude sur la rencontre de la pensée chrétienne avec la sagesse antique dans l'Hexaméron de Basile le Grand.* Paris.

Des Places, Edouard. 1976. *Platonismo e tradizione cristiana.* Ed. Pier Angelo Carozzi. Milan.

Dey, Lala Kalyan Kumar. 1975. *The Intermediary World and Patterns of Perfection in Philo and Hebrews.* Missoula, Mont.

Dörrie, Heinrich, Margarete Altenburger, and Uta Schramm, eds. 1976. *Gregor von Nyssa und die Philosophie.* Leiden.

Dürr, D. 1938. *Die Wertung des göttlichen Wortes im Alten Testament und im antiken Orient.* Leipzig.

Einstein, Albert. 1924. "Geleitwort" to *Lukrez von der Natur,* trans. Hermann Diels, ed. by Johannes Mewaldt. Berlin.

Faller, Otto. 1925. "Griechische Vergotung und christliche Vergöttlichung." *Gregorianum* 6:405–35.

Farandos, Georgios D. 1976. *Kosmos und Logos nach Philon von Alexandria.* Amsterdam.

Fleury, Eugène. 1938. *Hellénisme et christianisme: Saint Grégoire de Nazianze et son temps.* 2d ed. Paris.

Froidefond, Christian. 1971. *Le mirage égyptien dans la littérature grecque d'Homère à Aristote.* [Paris.]

Früchtel, Ursula. 1968. *Die kosmologischen Vorstellungen bei Philo von Alexandrien.* Leiden.

Gager, John G. 1972. *Moses in Greco-Roman Paganism.* Nashville.

Gale, Monica. 1994. *Myth and Poetry in Lucretius.* Cambridge.

Geffcken, Johannes. 1907. *Zwei griechische Apologeten.* Leipzig.

Gilson, Etienne. 1941. *God and Philosophy.* New Haven.

Giomini, Remo, ed. 1975. *M. Tulli Ciceronis scripta quae manserunt omnia,* 46. Leipzig.

Gloy, Karen. 1986. *Studien zur platonischen Naturphilosophie im Timaios.* Würzburg.

Grabmann, Martin. 1909. *Geschichte der scholastischen Methode.* 2 vols. Freiburg.

Gregg, Robert C. 1975. *Consolation Philosophy: Greek and Christian Paideia in Basil and the Two Gregories.* Cambridge, Mass.

Gronau, Karl. 1914. *Poseidonius und die jüdisch-christliche Genesisexegese.* Leipzig.

Gruber, Joachim. 1978. *Kommentar zu Boethius "De consolatione philosophiae,"* Berlin and New York.

Gunkel, Hermann. 1895. *Schöpfung und Chaos in Urzeit und Endzeit: Eine religionsgeschichtliche Untersuchung über Gen 1 und Ap Joh 12.* Göttingen.

Hamilton, Edith, and Huntington Cairns, eds. 1961. *The Collected Dialogues of Plato.* Bollingen Series. Princeton.

Harnack, Adolf von. 1901. *Das Wesen des Christentums.* 4th ed. Leipzig.

Heinisch, Paul. 1908. *Die griechische Philosophie im Buche der Weisheit.* Münster.

Hersey, George L. 1993. *High Renaissance Art in St. Peter's and the Vatican: An Interpretive Guide.* Chicago.

Hirsch, Walter. 1971. *Platons Weg zum Mythos.* Berlin.

Ivánka, Endre von. 1948. *Hellenisches und Christliches im frühbyzantinischen Geistesleben.* Vienna.

Jaeger, Werner. 1961. *Early Christianity and Greek Paideia.* Cambridge, Mass.

Jervell, Jacob. 1960. *Imago Dei: Gen. 1,26 f. im Spätjudentum, in der Gnosis und in den paulinischen Briefen.* Göttingen.

Jowett, Benjamin, ed. and trans. 1953. *The Dialogues of Plato.* 4th ed. 4 vols. Oxford.

Klibansky, Raymond. 1981. *The Continuity of the Platonic Tradition during the Middle Ages: Outlines of a "Corpus Platonicum Medii Aevi."* 2d ed. Munich.

Koch, Hal. 1932. *Pronoia und Paideusis.* Berlin.

Ladner, Gerhart B. 1959. *The Idea of Reform: Its Impact on Christian Thought and Action in the Age of the Fathers.* Cambridge, Mass.

Leonard, William Ellery, and Stanley Barney Smith, eds. 1942. *T. Lucretii Cari De rerum natura libri sex.* Madison.

Lerer, Seth. 1985. *Boethius and Dialogue: Literary Method in "The Consolation of Philosophy."* Princeton.

Lloyd, G.E.R. 1983. "Plato on Mathematics and Nature, Myth and Science." In International Christian University Publication IV-B, *Humanities: Christianity and Culture,* 11–30. Tokyo.

Lovejoy, Arthur O. 1936. *The Great Chain of Being: A Study of the History of an Idea.* Cambridge, Mass.

Mack, Burton L. 1972. "Imitatio Mosis: Patterns of Cosmology and Soteriology in the Hellenistic Synagogue." *Studia Philonica* 1:27–55.

———. 1973. *Logos und Sophia.* Göttingen.

Marcus, Ralph. 1945. "Jewish and Greek Elements in the LXX." In *Louis Ginzberg Jubilee Volume,* ed. Saul Lieberman et al., 227–45. New York.

Martin, Thomas Owen. 1951. "The Twenty-Eighth Canon of Chalcedon: A Background Note." In *Das Konzil von Chalkedon: Geschichte und Gegenwart,* ed. Aloys Grillmeier and Heinrich Bacht, 2:433–58. Würzburg.

Matter, Peter Paul. 1964. *Zum Einfluss des platonischen "Timaios" auf das Denken Plotins.* Winterthur.

May, Gerhard. 1994. *Creatio ex nihilo: The Doctrine of "Creation out of Nothing" in Early Christian Thought.* Trans. A.S. Worrall. Edinburgh.

McReynolds, Paul R. 1981. "John 1:18 in Textual Variation and Translation." In *New Testament Textual Criticism, Its Significance for Exegesis: Essays in Honor of Bruce M. Metzger,* ed. Eldon J. Epp and Gordon D. Fee, 105–18. Oxford.

Merlan, Philip. 1960. *From Platonism to Neoplatonism.* 2d ed. The Hague.

Mohr, Richard D. 1985. *The Platonic Cosmology.* Leiden.

Moulton, James Hope. 1957. *A Grammar of New Testament Greek: Prolegomena.* 3d ed., 1908. Reprint, Edinburgh.

Murray, John Courtney. 1964. *The Problem of God Yesterday and Today.* New Haven.

Nikiprowetzky, Valentin. 1977. *Le commentaire de l'Ecriture chez Philon d'Alexandrie.* Leiden.

Nock, Arthur Darby. 1962. "The Exegesis of *Timaeus* 28C." *Vigiliae Christianae* 16:79–86.

Norden, Eduard. 1924. *Die Geburt des Kindes.* Leipzig.

O'Brien, Denis Patrick. 1984. *Plato Weight and Sensation: The Two Theories of the "Timaeus."* Paris and Leiden.

O'Daly, Gerard. 1991. *The Poetry of Boethius.* London.

Ogilvie, Robert Maxwell. 1978. *The Library of Lactantius.* Oxford.

Pelikan, Jaroslav. 1971–89. *The Christian Tradition: A History of the Development of Doctrine.* 5 vols. Chicago.

———. 1990. "*Canonica Regula*: The Trinitarian Hermeneutics of Augustine." In *Collectanea Augustiniana,* ed. Joseph C. Schnaubelt and Frederick Van Fleteren, vol. 1, *Augustine: "Second Founder of the Faith,"* 329–43. New York.

———. 1993. *Christianity and Classical Culture: The Metamorphosis of Natural Theology in the Christian Encounter with Hellenism.* New Haven.

Pépin, Jean. 1964. *Théologie cosmique et théologie chrétienne (Ambroise, Exam. I, 1, 1–4).* Paris.

Pichon, René. 1901. *Lactance: Étude sur le mouvement philosophique et religieux sous le règne de Constantin.* Paris.

Pinault, Henri. 1925. *Le Platonisme de saint Grégoire de Nazianze: Essai sur les relations du Christianisme et de l'Hellenisme dans son oeuvre théologique.* La Roche-sur-Yon.

Prestige, George Leonard. 1956. *God in Patristic Thought.* London.

Raeder, Hans. 1905. *Platons philosophische Entwickelung.* Leipzig.

Reale, Giovanni. 1979. "Filone di Alessandria et la prima elaborazione filosofica della dottrina della creazione." In *Paradoxos Politeia: Studi patristici in onore di G. Lazzati,* ed. Raniero Cantalamessa and Luigi Franco Pizzolato, 247–87. Milan.

Reese, James M. 1970. *Hellenistic Influence on the Book of Wisdom and Its Consequences.* Rome.

Rivaud, Albert, ed. 1925. *Timée, Critias,* by Plato. Paris.

Rouse, William Henry Denham, and Martin Ferguson Smith, eds. 1992. *De rerum natura,* by Lucretius. Rev. ed. Cambridge, Mass.

Runia, David T. 1986. *Philo of Alexandria and the Timaeus of Plato.* Leiden.

Santayana, George. 1910. *Three Philosophical Poets. Lucretius, Dante, and Goethe.* Cambridge, Mass.

Sayre, Kenneth M. 1983. *Plato's Late Ontology: A Riddle Resolved.* Princeton.

Scheffel, Wolfgang. 1976. *Aspekte der platonischen Kosmologie: Untersuchungen zum Dialog "Timaios."* Leiden.

Scheible, Helga. 1972. *Die Gedichte in der Consolatio Philosophiae des Boethius.* Heidelberg.

Schulz, Dietrich Joachim. 1966. *Das Problem der Materie in Platons "Timaios."* Bonn.

Shorey, Paul. 1933. *What Plato Said.* Chicago.

———. 1938. *Platonism Ancient and Modern.* Berkeley.

Silk, Edward T. 1939. "Boethius's *Consolatio Philosophiae* as a Sequel to Augustine's Dialogues and Soliloquia." *Harvard Theological Review* 32:19–39.

Souter, Alexander J. 1910. "Chronicle of Patristica." *Journal of Theological Studies* 11:135–56.

Steck, Odil Hannes. 1981. *Der Schöpfungsbericht der Priesterschrift.* 2d ed. Göttingen.

Studer, Basil. 1995. "Zur Pneumatologie des Augustinus von Hippo (*De Trinitate* 15,17,27–27,50)." *Augustinianum* 35:567–83.

Switalski, Wladislaus. 1902. *Des Chalcidius Kommentar zu Plato's Timaeus: Eine historisch-kritische Untersuchung.* Münster.

Tarabochia Canavero, Alessandra. 1981. *Esegesi biblica e cosmologia: Note sull'interpretazione patristica e medioevale di Genesi 1,2.* Milan.

Tarán, L. 1972. "The Creation Myth in Plato's *Timaeus.*" In *Essays in Ancient Greek Philosophy,* ed. J.P. Anton and G.L. Hustas, 372–407. Albany, N.Y.

Taylor, Alfred Edward. 1928. *A Commentary on Plato's Timaeus.* Oxford.

Tcherikover, Avigdor. 1961. *Hellenistic Civilization and the Jews.* Trans. Shimon Applebaum. Philadelphia.

Theiler, Willy. 1971. "Philo von Alexandria und der hellenisierte *Timaeus.*" In *Philomathes: Studies and Essays in Memory of Philip Merlan,* ed. Robert B. Palmer and Robert Hamerton-Kelly, 25–35. The Hague.

Tigerstedt, Eugene Napoleon. 1974. *The Decline and Fall of the Neoplatonic Interpretation of Plato.* Helsinki.

Tobin, Thomas H. 1983. *The Creation of Man: Philo and the History of Interpretation.* Washington.

Troncarelli, Fabio. 1987. *Boethiana Aetas: Modelli grafici e fortuna manoscritta della "Consolatio Philosophiae" tra IX e XII secolo.* Alessandria.

Vignaux, Paul, ed. 1973. *In principio: Interprétations des premiers versets de la Genèse.* Paris.

Vlastos, Gregory. 1981. *Platonic Studies.* Princeton.

Vogel, Cornelia J. de. 1985. "Platonism and Christianity: A Mere Antagonism or a Profound Common Ground?" *Vigiliae Christianae* 39:1–62.

———. 1986. *Rethinking Plato and Platonism.* Leiden.

Von Rad, Gerhard. 1958. "Das theologische Problem des alttestamentlichen Schöpfungsglaubens." In *Gesammelte Studien zum Alten Testament,* 136–47. Munich.

Waszink, Jan Hendrik. 1964. *Studien zum Timaioskommentar des Calcidius.* Leiden.

———, ed. 1975. *Timaeus a Calcidio translatus commentarioque instructus.* 2d ed. London and Leiden.

Watts, Victor E., trans. 1969. Boethius. *The Consolation of Philosophy.* London and New York.

Weiss, H.F. 1966. *Untersuchungen zur Kosmologie des hellenistischen und palästinischen Judentums.* Berlin.

Wilken, Robert L., ed. 1975. *Aspects of Wisdom in Judaism and Early Christianity.* Notre Dame.

Williamson, Ronald. 1970. *Philo and the Epistle to the Hebrews.* Leiden.

Winden, J.C.M. van. 1959. *Calcidius on Matter: His Doctrine and Sources.* 2d ed. Leiden.

———. 1973. "The Early Christian Exegesis of 'Heaven and Earth' in *Genesis* 1.1." In *Romanitas et Christianitas: Festschrift J.H. Waszink,* ed. W. den Boer, 371–82. Amsterdam.

———. 1983. "The World of Ideas in Philo of Alexandria: An Interpretation of *De opificio mundi* 24–25." *Vigiliae Christianae* 37:209–17.

Winston, David. 1971. "The *Book of Wisdom's* Theory of Cosmogony." *History of Religions* 11, no. 2:185–202.

———. 1979. *The Wisdom of Solomon.* Garden City, N.Y.

———. 1992. "Solomon, Wisdom of." In *The Anchor Dictionary of the Bible,* ed. David Noel Freedman, 6:120–27. Garden City, N.Y.

Wolfson, Harry A. 1947. *Philo of Alexandria.* 2 vols. Cambridge, Mass.

———. 1956. *The Philosophy of the Church Fathers.* Cambridge, Mass.

Wortmann, Eberhard. 1965. *Das Gesetz des Kosmos: Die göttliche Harmonie nach Platons "Politeia"-"Timaios."* Remagen.

Yonge, C.D., ed. and trans. 1993. *The Works of Philo.* Rev. ed. Peabody, Mass.